THE
EXPAT

THE
EXPAT

**Powerful Life Lessons from Living, Working
and Traveling Around the World**

Jovelle Fernandez, M.D., Ph.D.

For more information: jovellefernandez@dr.com

ISBN: 979-8-88759-479-8

This book is dedicated to:

DADDY ALEX
My loving husband... my soulmate... my best friend

AJ
My first-born son... my inspiration
to zig while others are zagging

JUSTIN
My second son... my inspiration
to be better than my best

ALEX
My youngest son... my inspiration
to reflect and reward myself

MOCHI
My adorable shichon... my help to stop stressing out

Contents

Introduction

Congratulations on purchasing my book.

This book is all about my reflections and life lessons as an expatriate living in various countries for a significant period of my life. I was given the opportunity to be expatriated to Japan, Singapore, Belgium, and the U.S.A. This book also includes unforgettable experiences involving travels in select countries.

Of course, my family came along with me.

According to dictionary.com, an expatriate is a person who has moved from their native country to another country permanently or for an extended period. It most commonly refers to people who have chosen to relocate to work in a new country or to retire there. An expatriate is not the same as an immigrant since the former is associated with certain privileges. An expatriate is loosely referred to as an expat.

Was the attractive relocation package enough for me to choose to be expatriated? Just thinking about the idea sends tingles to my toes, urging me to dance. Was it the intense enthusiasm that my family and I would have the chance to explore other countries? I believe I had an insatiable appetite that there was something out there bigger than the pond that I was swimming in. Jokoy, a famous Filipino American comedian, mentioned, "Just keep following your damn dreams ..." and I guess that is what I did! That is what my family did!

Obviously, curiosity lurked. We had to pause and examine everything around us, as we did when we revisited the sets of "Game of Thrones" in Croatia or examined the wide array of art displayed at the Louvre in Paris. Because we also learned another language, sometimes we use a language that only we think we will understand and that others around us will not. This came in handy when we negotiated in the flea markets of Thailand and Vietnam or agreed amongst ourselves about which food to order in Greece and Montenegro.

We had tons of fun! Like over-the-top swag! Moreover, frequent travels led me to achieve airline million miler and hotel elite status.

There were times when we were uneasy as well. More of a panic attack for me. I was trembling and perspiring heavily when I was almost victimized in the streets of London during one of my business travels.

Come to think of it, if you were me, how would you respond to a handsome Chris Hemsworth look-alike guy who is nude and asks you to massage his back? Hmm... would you run away from this seemingly harmless gentleman? Remember, by a look-alike, I was referring to the Thor image and all.

What would you do if suddenly, out of nowhere, a baby girl is thrown at your lap by a mother pleading with you to take her child for a better future? Would you be compassionate enough and take that child with you? Would you get carried away by your emotion and basic instinct as a mother?

And how important is foreplay? This is not for adults' only kind of foreplay.

These and several other stories will amaze you as to how surprising encounters lead to a lot of "aha" moments and learnings. They made me who I am today and who my family is today. Certain realities in life opened my eyes and changed my perspective differently altogether. These stories will forever linger in my mind because they challenged my core values, questioned my beliefs, and, most importantly, enabled me to become closer to my family and deepened my faith in God.

Living as a foreigner has its unique challenges. Being alienated has its special constraints.

While remote working is becoming the standard, we still constantly struggle to try to understand what is out there beyond where we are living and working comfortably right now. Even if we do our communication virtually at times, we may have that never-ending question in our minds to try to understand the whys. Why was the behavior like that? Why was the response like that? Sometimes, we also wonder whether there is another place for us somewhere out there—a place where we can experience the perks similar to an expat, a place where we can develop and become better than our best selves.

Hold that restlessness and wait no further... as this book may help you know more, learn more, and understand more about being away from one's comfort zone and learnings from whatever comes along with it. You may also benefit if you are feeling like you do not belong in a certain way, even if you are and want to stay in your own comfort zone.

This book will reveal the life lessons of an expat who lived in five countries and traveled in fifty of them. This book will teach you how to discover certain realities in life that you may not be aware of yet. You do not need to be expatriated in the real sense of the word to apply the techniques that I will share in this book.

This book will assure you how to be okay with not being included and how the word "inclusive" may be overrated in the workplace. How to always arm yourself with your core values, as those are important tools for you to survive.

I applied those in the actual experiences. I succeeded and emerged as a winner.

I am going to reveal those life lessons to you.

Because you will succeed, too!

And you can be a winner!

So, wonderful citizens of the world, read on and learn more about the Nude Guy!

You need to keep on reading to realize the value of The Foreplay!

CHAPTER ONE

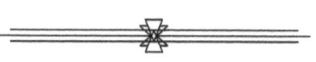

The Nude Guy

Germany

I had travelled and stayed in Germany several times, made connecting flights at Frankfurt, Munich, and Dusseldorf, and even got stranded due to inclement weather a couple of times. Germany is a beautiful country with mostly English-speaking locals.

In fact, I had to learn some of the German words in Japan when I had a special license to practice medicine there. In the clinics in Japan, some of the medical lingoes are in German, not just Japanese. In addition, the person who gave me a shot in the pharmaceutical industry and patiently mentored me, who till this day gives me career advice, is a German physician. I have several German friends as well. I always exchange notes with my brother, Jon, when he travels to Germany for business.

In other words, with all these factors, I thought I already had some sense of understanding about Germany and a certain familiarity involving the country and its people. That's what I thought ...

Hence, you can imagine how it must have been for me when I had the encounter with the nude guy.

Let me tell you that story.

Business meetings can be stressful and taxing at times. I make it a habit to de-stress myself. Whenever I get the chance, what I usually do is head towards the gym and do my exercise while listening to Nicole Scherzinger's music. Sometimes, I just sit idly in the hotel lounge while listening to songs of internationally renowned Filipinos, Lea Salonga, Arnel Pineda, and Martin Nievera. But I am not brave enough to explore new territories on my own. So, if I walk outside the hotel, make a food trip, visit tourist spots, or go to the spa, I usually tag somebody with me.

The story of the nude guy happened during the last day of the meeting when most of the attendees had already left after the meeting was over. Travel between Europe and Asia was not easy during that time; hence, options were fairly limited. Most of us who needed to board flights to Asia were the ones who had to stay behind for another night.

I was able to convince a colleague to go to the spa of the hotel. We had a spa coupon, and we did not want to waste it. The spa of the hotel was located in the basement, and the men's and women's spas were on the same floor.

We were already done bathing, changed into our outdoor clothes, and were doing whatever women do after a shower or bath. In hindsight, thank goodness we were already in that phase. We were discussing how the meeting went and what to do next. Just a side note, business meetings never stop. They can happen anywhere, even in the spa. We just need to be careful that confidential matters are not discussed openly.

Suddenly, out of nowhere, a Caucasian guy in his maybe early 30s showed up. Poof! Almost like a Greek god that descended and showed himself to his human constituents. He asked us if we were interested in massaging his back because he couldn't reach it. Mind you, he was nude, totally nude. He was good-looking and well-chiseled. Just imagine yourself taking an art class with a nude guy in front of you as your subject. That was how the scene looked like. There were just no easels in between. And close enough, less than the physical distancing required to avoid COVID-19 transmission.

And he was like Thor. Remember the scene from the movie "Thor: Love and Thunder" when Thor was in front of Zeus and was magically undressed? And the ladies fainted after that? That must have been how I felt or how my colleague felt. Or maybe, how both of us felt. I never asked her about it.

My colleague was just staring at the mirror and didn't utter a word. She turned pale, and just stood there frozen. I guess she did not know what to do or how to respond. Like a scene where you can hear a pin drop because everything was at a standstill.

My heart was thumping heavily in my chest, and my mind was totally blank. I was speechless and motionless for a few minutes.

Hmmm... for some reason, a miraculous, powerful force brought me back to reality, and I was able to think. There in front of me was this beautiful creature. I had a flashback of a friend's bridal party, with all of us having a good time. Well, I might as well feast my eyes with a free live show. Bad girl ...What was I thinking?

I stared at the guy from head to toe and stopped at the toe. That may have been a lame attempt to hide my flushed face. Then I went back up again to stare at his face.

Was he just an exhibitionist? Did he think we were "easy" Asian girls that he could just pick up? Was that his pick-up line?

Pick-up line... I prefer Joey's from my favorite sitcom, "Friends," which is "How you doin'?"

Come back to your senses, Jovelle. Think... Keep your eyes focused on the face... don't move them further down. Think hard! Oops... not hard. Think objectively!

I used my peripheral vision to locate anything that might have been useful during that situation—trying to recall where the exit was, which I couldn't remember anymore. I usually do not have a good sense of direction anyway. Where was the telephone? Where was the button that you needed to press in case of emergency? Or maybe, I couldn't think clearly because I was too distracted by this nude guy in front of me.

Was he hiding a weapon with him?

Was he alone? Were there other people in the spa during that time?

Did he look like a villain? Like a deceitful Loki of the Avengers? Would he put my colleague and me in danger? Would he be able to take both of us? Would somebody hear us if we shouted for help?

Darn... I should have taken judo or karate lessons while in Japan for nearly eight years prior to that. That might have given me some confidence to confront him.

For some reason, I cannot recall how I regained my composure and tried my best to show no interest in this hunk. I forgot how I bravely uttered the words, "We are done. We are about to leave."

The nude guy looked frustrated. With his arms folded in his chest, he expressed German words of disbelief. Maybe just maybe, he was thinking, "Look at me, the most good-looking man in Germany. And you are not interested? Seriously?"

He dropped both of his hands by his side and just said, "Okay." Then he left.

Thank God it was over.

I guess I was still recovering from that shock with my eyes open wide, jaw dropped, and standing there staring blankly at the wall. My colleague was still not moving. I knew I had to tell her to hurry up and that both of us had to get our things and leave the place.

The devil side of me was whispering things that I made the wrong decision because I let that situation pass. When I told that story to other lady friends, they said I must be crazy to let go of a once-in-a-lifetime opportunity. They kept on saying that if you are presented with an opportunity, you must grab it and never let it go. What do you ladies think?

The angel side of me was calming me down because it was over. My angel was giving me assurance that I made the right choice. I guess this is aligned with what the partners and other gentlemen would think.

Was it really over?

Nope.

There is more to this story.

The nude guy returned. Yes, he returned. Still the same guy, still nude, still asking for the same favor. "Can you join me at the spa and massage my back?" This time, I didn't hear it as a request but more of a command. This time, while he was saying it, he was sort of walking back and forth as if he was a model of underwear sans the underwear. Hmm... typical exhibitionist.

The devil side of me appeared victorious. "Hurray! I knew it. C'mon Jovelle... grab the chance. Not everyone is given a second chance." The angel side of me was shaking her head. "Oh no, Jovelle. Don't let this devil lure you to the depths of hell."

Well, the second time around, I was more courageous and was already back to my senses.

I was no longer affected by this nude guy, no matter how devilishly handsome he looked.

That feeling of being rattled already passed. Or not?

I am happily married to my personal hunk, and for me, he is the most good-looking, perfect, and kindest gentleman in the whole universe. The important thing is he does not censure me with my seemingly unacceptable married woman comments every time I watch movies of Tom Cruise. Hence, no restrictions for giggles for handsome-looking guys. Because I was never inhibited from expressing my feelings in dreamland, it may have helped me with my behavior involving reality. It helped me manage my decorum involving the nude guy.

Armed with that strong love for my husband, the conservative culture of being a Filipino coupled with faith in God as a devout Catholic, I composed myself and replied firmly to the nude guy.

I said, "Believe it or not, our husbands are waiting for us upstairs, and they must be worried by now. We are not interested."

The nude guy shook his head in disbelief and left.

My colleague and I left the spa immediately after that and barely spoke a word until we arrived at the hotel lobby.

You know what? It was true that our husbands were waiting for us in the lobby. They arrived that day to join us for a short holiday before heading back to Asia. We shared the story, and we all dissolved into laughter and uncontrollably cried at the same time. My husband chuckled and mentioned that we may have regretted not doing the nude guy the favor he asked. While laughing out loud, my colleague's husband joked and said that we may have responded differently if the husbands were not there.

Seriously, my husband was very grateful that I behaved like that. The thought of being harmed during that situation did not escape him, though.

Well, there you go. A great story to tell, and the two couples had a great bond after that.

Great stories create long-lasting friendships.

Speaking of spas.

For those of you who have tried onsen or public baths in Japan, people do enter the bath wearing nothing; at least there is something. And that something is a piece of a small towel. In other countries where I tried their spas, there is something, which is usually a bathing suit. Hammam spa in Turkey is uniquely different, though. Hammam spa includes washing, traditional body scrubbing with *kese*, a foam wash, and a massage. Just the thought of it makes me wish to travel back to Istanbul.

Back to the onsen, you can imagine what it must have been like for me when I entered for the first time. It was challenging to be told to take off all my clothes, and the only situation I have ever used or heard of that is during a physical health examination. I was told to leave all clothes and bags inside a locker and just bring a small towel inside the spa.

During that time, I was not that fluent in the Japanese language yet. I did not know what to do with the small towel, despite receiving instructions in Japanese. What would I do with the small towel? Would I cover my face so that if they saw me outside of the onsen, I would not be recognized? Would I use it to cover a part of my body and avoid exposing anything I did not want to be seen?

There is a saying that goes like this, "Learn to sit back and observe."

That is what I did. I did not know what to do with the small towel, so I observed. If you do not know what to do with something, just watch and learn.

I stayed a bit behind and observed what the Japanese women did with the towel. They used it to rub their body to get rid of dirt while taking a quick shower before dipping themselves in the water. They used the small towel to wrap their hair over their heads when they took a dip. Talk about cleanliness and orderliness to the highest level.

The males are separate from females when nude unless you are in a couple's spa.

I learned my lesson involving the small towel.

But what about the nude guy? I am still having difficulty understanding what transpired in Germany with the nude guy.

What if he just needed help to massage his back?

What if he genuinely needed to be massaged because of a medical condition?

Well, until today, the what-ifs never ended.

Come to think of it, the what-ifs usually come to our minds when we are confronted with a situation where we need to make decisions. Decisions to say something or behave in a certain way. There is no hard and fast rule on how to approach challenging situations. I must say that we should be guided by our values and have foresight on the impact of our actions or behavior. We need to follow our instincts and listen to that inner, hopefully right, voice. Sometimes fight or flight comes into play as well, especially if we are in a potentially dangerous situation.

In that nude guy situation, I had tools. I was guided by my instinct and values.

Instinct to examine my environment in case my safety or that of my colleague would be compromised. Instinct to always watch my back because I was raised in the Philippines, where the crime rate was relatively high at one per one thousand.[1]

Values when I exchanged vows of marriage that I made with my husband that I hold sacred. Values involving my Catholic faith, since I was raised as a Catholic to a certain extreme level that all my brothers Joel, Jon, Joseph, and Jai were educated in the seminary.

Were those tools enough to manage the nude guy situation? At least my colleague and I came out from that situation scathe-free.

What do you think?

---

[1]   https://www.statista.com/topics/6994/crime-in-the-philippines/#dossierKeyfigures

CHAPTER TWO

Three Minutes

Belgium

As an expat, you will receive a lot of perks. There is a long list of tangible benefits. This includes travel and accommodation, among others. There is relocation assistance to have the household goods shipped, so packing our stuff was not much of a challenge, so much so that we got used to having our heirlooms and other pieces of furniture with us wherever we lived. We just needed to ensure we had itemized inventory, which included what boxes the items were placed in, which room they originated to be packed in, and which room they would be unpacked at the destination. It was an exuberant indifference since the process can go into some detail, but at the same time, that eagerness to be in a new place loomed. It wasn't perfect all the time and had some challenges as well concerning damaged goods during shipment. But that is another story.

As a foreigner, one needs to learn a lot of new things, and this is not just limited to the language. It can also be as simple as understanding how dates are written. For example, in Japan, you need to know the year that denotes the reign of the emperor and its equivalent ordinary year, followed by month and day. Belgium is similar to Singapore. It starts with the day first, followed by the month and year. As simple as the date can be confusing since forms need to be filled out and the shelf lives of food items need to be known. Remember that infamous food poisoning scene of "The Bridesmaids" where the entire bridal party had diarrhea and vomiting? It was hysterically entertaining to watch, but I bet you do not want to experience that.

I got expatriated to Belgium from Singapore. Obviously, the family was so excited. Europe is known to have a very rich history and culture. Belgium is an advanced country. We travelled to Europe every now and then and are very familiar with Belgium.

We loved the countless varieties of waffles. There are so many types of beers! And ooh... the chocolates. As a self-proclaimed dessert connoisseur, I dare say that Belgian chocolates are the best in the world.

We were so amazed by the wonderful sights, such as the flower carpet in Brussels during the summer. Our faith was strengthened when we went to Leuven, where the bodily relics of one of the venerated saints, Father Damien, the leper priest, is located. We learned countless myths and legends and walked through so many bridges in Bruges. We had the chance to explore the origin of the Congregation of the Immaculate Heart of Mary or CICM missionaries, the group that established the university where my husband and I studied and met.

These and other countless other beauties of Belgium make it an enticing country to live in.

Belgium is multicultural and multilingual, with the Dutch-speaking Flemish community and the French-speaking Wallonia. We stayed at a French community or commune because that was closer to my place of work and the international school where our son got accepted. We got settled in quite quickly despite the chilly and gloomy winter season when we arrived.

At least, that is what we thought.

Well, well... traveling to Europe is not the same as living and working in Europe.

We had to explain to our youngest son that Santa Claus did not come to Belgium. There is St. Nicholas, who goes to malls on the sixth of December. It was not good enough for him since he got used to the image of Santa Claus found in the "Miracle on 34th Street" kind. My sister, Joy, who was living in the U.S., was frustrated when she visited us since she had to pay for condiments provided by fast food restaurants and pay when she used the public toilets. And we were so conscious of our trash since we had to pay for its disposal.

At least during that time, we needed to figure out a way to do our groceries because the grocery stores were only open during office hours. There were very few grocery or small shops, far from where we lived, that were open beyond office hours or during weekends and holidays. Our after-office hours and weekends were no longer spent inside grocery stores and shopping malls but with family and taking strolls at the parks.

We hardly found Asians living there or even Asian stores.

Transportation was not as convenient as in Japan or Singapore. A car is needed to move around. It gets extremely cold and snowy during the winter, and every day, you need to bring an umbrella because it usually rains.

A tangible part of the Belgium relocation package was a company car. In order to be issued a company car, I needed to have a local driver's license. In order to get a driver's license, I needed to take both written and practical exams in French because I lived in a French commune. The absolute priority to the right was a bit confusing. You may say we nailed it because we were issued driver's licenses. But, actually, my husband and I were given exemptions. Kudos to the Philippine embassy!

Of course, I took several practical driving tests. I had to take a practical exam before being issued a company car in the Philippines. But there was no language hurdle there, just the traffic along EDSA in Manila. I had to take another one when we moved to the U.S. There was no language issue there either; I just had to develop the skill of parallel parking and silently count for a few seconds on a stop sign.

Of course, we made friends in the office and outside the office as well. We met a Filipino family in the church but lost contact since we left.

Working there was another challenge. I am used to working hard and sometimes too hard, and I lose track of time. Somebody told me at one point not to hire a hard-working Filipino. Another asked me why I had an office, and she didn't have one. I just shrugged with both of my eyebrows pulled down, my nose wrinkled, and my upper lip pulled up.

Thinking of hard-working Filipino, was I just trying to show off?

Or was it because, as a foreigner, I needed to excel and do more to be recognized?

I felt alone at the office. My family felt alone living there. We were overwhelmed with the new environment yet indifferent for not really having a firm grasp of what was around us. That feeling of discomfort was so intense that sometimes I unconsciously tapped my foot.

Because of these challenges, we had to make the most of what we had. There were privileges, of course, such as French language lessons and others. We lived in a big three-story, four-bedroom house with a den in the basement and a big garden with apricot and apple fruit trees. We had a lot of opportunities to travel and sometimes just drive to the neighboring European countries every time we got the chance. We had everything we needed and wanted and much more.

So, what more could we ask for?

Speaking of the house.

It was summer, and we had to travel. My husband and our youngest son traveled to Singapore to pick up our two older sons for relocation to Belgium. I had a business trip during that time to Japan and the U.S., and we all met in Amsterdam and then took the flight to Belgium.

When the five of us arrived at our house, my heart went up to my mouth, and I broke into a cold sweat.

The front door and windows were open. Kitchen utensils and clothes were on the floor. Everything was topsy-turvy. Many valuables were missing.

We were burglarized!

There was even a hole in the bathtub.

I called my assistant, who called the police. We were so exhausted because of the long trip, and we just stood in the hallway with all our bags unpacked. We did not touch anything. I guess I watch too many crime stories.

Two policemen arrived, and they looked at us and asked, "*Parlai Francais*?" Meaning, "Do you speak French?"

I responded, "*Je parle un petit peu de Francais*," stating that I only speak a little French.

They went around the big house and left after three minutes.

Three minutes.

Nothing else was done. No other questions were asked. No conversation transpired after that. They just left. My mind was reeling. My eyes rolled as I was having difficulty processing the events.

What just happened?

We had never felt so helpless. We had never felt so afraid. We hugged each other, and the reality struck us... we did not belong there.

I thought moving to another place outside our comfort zone would enrich our lives as we learned a new culture and a new language and as we visited other places. I love European culture because it is so rich. I love learning French because it sounds romantic. I love Europe because of its amazing architecture and scenery. I thought we would be happy there.

Excitement was replaced by fear.

Happiness was replaced by isolation.

My definition of happiness is simple—peace of mind. And my peace of mind meter is to be able to sleep peacefully at night.

I have never felt safe after that. Since that event, I always go around the house to double-check the locks and the windows. Just the sound of neighbor's dogs barking at night makes me tremble. Even the ruffle of the leaves of the trees wakes me up. My hands become cold and clammy behind the wheel when I see individuals who cross the road and appear suspicious. Were they the ones who burglarized our house?

When I shared the story with my colleagues, I was taken aback by their reactions. Of course, they were remorseful that we were victimized, but the news came as no surprise to them. Apparently, during summer, when people leave their homes for vacation, there is already an expectation that one's house will be burglarized. Some of them never bother to lock their doors or close their windows because it would be more expensive to replace locks or shattered windows. They just leave whatever items are of small value for thieves to take. One important thing is that the prisons are already crowded. Simple burglary or theft does not get much attention from the police as they have more important crimes to pursue, like heinous ones.

They told me that I would never be able to trace my pieces of jewelry and that they were already redesigned into something else. Hence, I should give up because there is no way for me to retrieve the family heirlooms that were stolen. I should have had my pieces of jewelry insured before moving to Belgium.

Come to think of it. The day before we left the country, a stranger knocked at our door, telling us that his son's ball had accidentally landed in our garden. We did not find any. During that time, our bags were in the hallway since we had an early flight the next day. Was that the guy who burglarized our house? Did he know we would be out? Maybe he saw our bags in the hallway?

With every expatriation, I usually have integration into the country, such as learning dos and don'ts and things that I need to be aware of. I was not told that during summer, if you leave your home, burglary is so high. My French teacher did not teach me how to explain myself in French if I am victimized by burglary. I was only taught about it after I experienced the unfortunate event.

Was critical information such as the crime rate not shared because I never asked? Was it to entice people to relocate to another country; hence the "not-so-good" side of such a country would never be told? Was it because I assumed I would be told about the negative aspects of a country before expatriating? Was it because I was expected to know more about the country myself rather than expect it to come from the relocation package?

Because the French language was associated with burglary, I lost interest in learning French after that, which was not fair. Goodbye to *La vie en rose* solo singing on my bucket list.

Because my pieces of jewelry were stolen, I began to dislike Belgium after that, which was also not fair. I had to strike a balance between maintaining my good relationship with my Belgian friends and my agnostic feeling toward Belgium.

The burglary was so ironic! Can you imagine me, originally from the Philippines, being victimized in another country?

The sad part was I never had my valuables insured. For me, and I guess some of you, and for most Filipinos, that was not the norm.

Glass half full... The most important part was that none of us were harmed.

Speaking of feeling of helplessness, there is another story where we got caught up with the intricacies of a country with varied political views.

There was one time when we left Belgium and travelled by plane to London to watch football. My two older sons are such big fans of Arsenal and Real Madrid. It was just a short trip. Upon our return, our youngest son's residency card was questioned by the immigration officer. Apparently, it was registered in the French commune, and his residency card had no picture on it, so it was considered unacceptable. Was that a request for us to swerve? I felt cold spiderlike fingers crawling up and down my spine as we were escorted to a room full of foreigners with questionable entry documents. We were asked to wait in a room while the immigration officer figured that one out and then decided to let us in or not. That was a real blower because his card was issued by the officials of the country from the community where we were living. The difference is that it was not issued by the same office as the one in Brussels because we were not living in that community.

Hmmm... How would I know that the card issued by the French commune was not considered official by the Flemish immigration officer? Was it my fault that both French and Flemish communes have their own rules that they were not recognized by the other even though they are all living in one country with a little over eleven million population?[2] Who am I to question the decision of the immigration officer for us not to be allowed to enter, despite having legal documents to enter and stay?

We were finally allowed to enter the country after a couple of hours.

We had to bounce before the immigration officer changed his mind.

And that is not the only unforgettable story with passport control and immigration. With so many international travels, I have other stories to share. And you may shake your head further in disbelief because

---

[2] https://www.belgium.be/en/about_belgium/tourism

they happened in the Philippines, with my Philippine passport.

The first incident involved a trip from Japan. When it was my turn to meet the immigration officer, I was surprised by his comments.

"So, you came from Japan. What did you do there?"

I mentioned I was doing my post-graduate degree and was doing clinical practice.

"Really? There is such a thing? Are you sure you are not *Japayuki*? I have not heard of a situation like yours in Japan." He said this while grinning and, at the same time, shaking his head in disbelief. So rude!

Instead of being offended because of how he labeled me since the context of *Japayuki* is demeaning as it refers to women working at bars or nightclubs, I responded, "Thank you, sir. I actually consider it as a compliment. Because that means I am young, beautiful, and sexy."

His face turned red as if he had been slapped in the face several times by the Ant-Man, and he allowed me to enter without any other additional questions.

Maybe that was the velvet hammer in me who responded, saying to him how insane his remarks were without using the word insane or anything similar to it. Or maybe because I did not want my excitement to be dampened by a trivial encounter. Read on to find out more about the velvet hammer.

The second incident was more complex, and that was leaving the Philippines for a trip to South Korea, Australia, and then to the UK. And because I was using a Philippine passport during that time, I needed visas to travel to those countries. Because I travel a lot, I have several passports together, with the passport on top having more pages to be stamped by immigration officers and the other passports with unexpired visas.

You can just imagine how the immigration officer's jaw dropped when he was handed several passports stapled together while leaving the country and shown a flight itinerary that seemed endless.

He scratched his head and asked what I do. I mentioned that I am a physician and work in a pharmaceutical company.

"Why do you have to travel to many countries?"

Because... duh. That was just in my head. I responded politely that part of my job is doing scientific activities in many countries.

He asked for my overseas Filipino worker card. I could not show any because my employment was an intercompany transfer. He did not understand what that meant. My situation was not the same as a usual overseas Filipino worker.

He said he couldn't let me through because I had incomplete documents. He told me to go to the overseas Filipino worker's office, which is in another city. I was required to apply for a card and show that card to him. Then and only then would I be allowed to leave the country. He even told all his fellow immigration officers working at that time not to let me fall in line in their booths except with his booth because he should be the one to manage my case. Wow... drag me!

What that meant was that I would miss my flights. I would miss my meetings.

I never expected that, with my frequent travels, I would not be allowed to leave a country. And that country was my country of origin. I did not know what to do at that time. It is rare for me to depend on others if I have an issue that I need to solve. But during that time, I knew it was out of my control. I used a helpline. I called a lawyer friend who was working at the foreign affairs office at that time. She told me what to do. She also informed me that the demand of the immigration officer was unreasonable and that she would use this incident to educate them.

She told me to go back to that same immigration officer and that she would talk to him.

I did what she told me. I was already being paged, and an airline employee was calling for my name at the immigration line as the plane was scheduled to leave. I had to rush to catch my flight and tripped several times. I was able to catch my flight and made it to my meetings. Hallelujah!

That may have been one of the reasons why I had to undergo knee surgery at one point.

My story involving the airport doesn't end there. This time, it involves three minutes.

For those of you who have been to Barcelona, it is a challenge to navigate the airport and find the airport lounge. One time, I was searching for it, and a good-looking, seemingly familiar gentleman just behind me was doing the same. He must have noticed my boarding pass, so he was just following me. I finally found the place, and the gentleman also followed suit.

While he was seated across from where I settled myself, I had a better glimpse of his appearance. He was in one of the movies that I watched on the plane on my way there. The movie was "Bridget Jones's Baby." And yes, the good-looking gentleman was Patrick Dempsey.

But you know what? Maybe my eyes were gleaming with amazement during that time that I even forgot his name. Can you imagine what sort of memory lapse that was, considering that I just watched his movie? I guess that happens.

He looked gentle and kind. So, when both of us were standing at the buffet area, and after ordering a waffle, I took the courage to start a conversation with him.

"Do you happen to be a Hollywood actor?" What a silly question, Jovelle! I couldn't think of anything else to say at the time.

"Yes, mam," he answered with a smile.

"That's what I thought. I just watched 'Bridget Jones's Baby' on the plane."

"So, what do you think about it?" he asked.

"You did great," I responded in a high-pitched voice. Perhaps still star-struck that Patrick was talking to me.

"Hmmm ..." just to normalize my voice. "I didn't like the ending, though. It would have been a good twist if you ended up with Bridget Jones, right?" I said in my normal tone of voice.

"Yeah, I am with you on that!" he chuckled.

"Indeed," I responded while holding my phone.

He must have sensed that I was about to ask him to have a picture together, so he volunteered to take our selfie.

We exchanged a few more pleasantries after that and talked about "Grey's Anatomy" as well. Good thing I had some sense of the TV series since I prefer to watch legal dramas like "Suits" than those with medical plots. Otherwise, I may not have maintained the conversation for three minutes.

And yes, the conversation lasted for three minutes because I was told by the chef that my waffle should be ready in three minutes.

The importance of three minutes ...

I did not realize until recently that my youngest son, Alex, felt confused about his origin growing up. I only knew about it when I read his essay while he was in middle school at American School in Japan. He was born in Japan, educated in international schools in Singapore and Belgium, and studied as well at one of the best public schools in Pennsylvania, U.S. Because we relocated frequently, he had no constant friends while growing up. He had difficulty with his origin living in various countries, but he is very passionate about learning about the culture and history of the Philippines. He finally realized what his name meant— "defender, protector." He really upholds that name because he stands up for what he believes in. Before that, I did not know that, to a certain degree, just like me, he also struggled to live in another country.

And I never even noticed that. I was so engrossed with my career to prove to others around me that I was highly capable.

If I had spent a few moments with my son just to tell him stories about the Philippines, about our culture, perhaps he would have understood his origin earlier, and perhaps he would not have struggled with it. Just like what I did with my two older sons, maybe even three minutes a day could have helped, just one short story. Just maybe ...

I became too preoccupied with the idea that living in another country had more rewards and benefits rather than challenges.

We became much closer as a family after our relocation to Belgium. It took a burglary incident for me to realize my role in the household because after that unfortunate incident, I spent more quality time with my family. It took a burglar for me to understand that I needed to pay attention to my husband and our three sons. We were bound closer by the unfortunate burglary incident and realized that at the end of the day, the ones that we have are each other.

Lessons learned.

I nearly forgot the hole in the bathtub. Apparently, valuables are stored underneath the bathtub in Belgium. For some reason, the burglars didn't notice from the big pictures in the hallway that the residents were from Asia. We even had our flag displayed. Maybe they didn't know the flag of the Philippines?

Speaking of holes ...

CHAPTER THREE

Poke a Hole in the Wall

India, Part One

My previous roles in the corporate world necessitated a lot of traveling. I was traveling seventy percent of the time due to business.

I love to travel. In fact, that was one of my wishes during one of my birthdays when I was growing up. Don't get me wrong. I am not a boujee. I thought that it was so cool to travel and see wonderful places.

India was one of the countries that I frequently visited.

My experiences involving trips to India spanned a wide spectrum. I cried with pity and sadness since I had seen extremes of poverty in Mumbai. I was lavished with the best service and slept like a queen in New Delhi. My Catholic faith was strengthened when I visited the tomb of Mother Theresa in Calcutta a couple of times.

I felt like a famous person when I was escorted by three of my former colleagues when I had a meeting in Patna.

I am not a big fan of spicy food, though. Talk about another way to lose weight. This is something that I always look forward to, given that most of my travels add to my weight.

I had a former mentor who jokingly told me that a visit to India is like fulfilling my dream to be working at the World Health Organization (WHO). He had so much faith in me that he gave me an opportunity to work with WHO experts and published a bulletin in the field of vaccination. I never saw any disbelief in his eyes regarding my capability. Never did he have any bias that I would not be able to do an important job.

It was India that taught me important lessons about biases and expectations.

I was staying at the hotel venue of the academic meeting, and I was supposed to give a talk the following day. I had a long-haul flight and needed to charge my phone. So where was the electrical outlet? Surely there must have been one somewhere. I tried my best to look for it, but I couldn't find one. The room was also dimly lit, so I gave up looking. I figured that I might have just been exhausted and missed it, or I was not trying hard enough to look for it. What is the purpose of the hotel guest services anyway?

I was expecting that the hotel personnel from the other end would tell me where to plug my phone charger. However, he said that he would send an electrician to come up to my room.

That's strange. Maybe there was a fuse or circuit breaker somewhere that needed to be turned on? Maybe the source of the light was not the same as that of the electric outlet?

In a few minutes, a tall, dark skinny guy wearing an undershirt and shorts and holding a screwdriver knocked at my door. I began to perspire heavily with both hands clenched because of how he looked, the clothes he wore, and the tool he was holding.

He introduced himself as the hotel electrician.

Unbelievable ...

An employee of the highest-rated hotel in that town wearing an undershirt and shorts with no name tag. Really?

I called hotel guest services again. I described the man outside my door, and I received confirmation that he was their electrician. My head was throbbing, and I continuously rubbed my forehead, hoping to be eased of my misery while talking with the hotel guest services personnel. I mentioned that it was unacceptable for them to send a guy looking like that—holding a screwdriver—and allow him to enter my room. His response had been consistent—that he was the best electrician in that town. He reminded me again that it was already past office hours. I needed to let him in as soon as possible because he needed to address another electrical problem in the meeting area of the hotel. If I didn't let him in, I would never be able to charge any of my devices. It took time for the hotel personnel to convince me. I can be a nag at times, but what the *shongers* (slang for insane situation that my BFF's and I use)? I gave up. My head was floating, and words were not coming out of my mouth anymore.

Would you believe that I did let the electrician in? But of course, I kept the door ajar and just stayed beside it while holding my purse with my passport and wallet.

Anyway, the next thing that happened blew my mind. My eyes were wide open the entire time, and my entire body became so stiff that Medusa may have cast a spell on me.

He poked a hole in the wall using the screwdriver he was holding, pulled out the wires, peeled the covering of the wires to expose them, and asked for my charger with a hand gesture, pointing at the charger on top of the bedside table.

Ahh, so that was the purpose of the screwdriver.

Nothing to be afraid of here. But hold on, live wires from the hole in the wall?

I was a bit reluctant to hand over my charger to him since I was not sure whether I would be electrocuted or whether he would be electrocuted when I handed it to him. I figured that maybe, just maybe, he was used to it and developed some sort of "electrocution tolerance." Is there such a thing?

I started walking slowly as if traversing through a thick pile of mud that every step was so tedious to make. I got hold of a small towel, wrapped my charger with it, and handed the charger to him.

He connected the live wires to my charger, and viola... my phone was already charging. He was so pleased with what he did and gave me a smile and left the room.

I just stood there. I did not know for how long. I was still trying to process what I had just witnessed.

Screwdriver... poked a hole in the wall... pulled out the wires... connected to my charger.

Screwdriver... poked a hole in the wall... pulled out the wires... connected to my charger.

The scene kept playing on and on in my head.

I came back to my senses when the hotel phone rang. Hotel personnel at the other end asked if my problem was resolved. I said it was. I did not tell him how the problem was solved. I did not tell him because I sensed he was not interested in listening further. Or maybe I was struggling to share the story and couldn't find the right words.

Why didn't I give a chance to this guy when I was already given assurance as to who he was? I remained so skeptical about his capability because of how he dressed up. He was clearly capable because he was able to resolve the situation. He helped me with my problem. It did not matter what he wore or what he used to solve the problem. The important thing was that he did it! The important thing was that my phone was charged.

If my former mentor acted the same way that I did involving the hotel electrician, would I be given a shot at the WHO? And to make matters worse, I came directly from academia and clinical practice. I did not have much experience during that time with supranational organizations such as the WHO. Yet, he trusted me.

If I had trusted the electrician immediately to do his thing, without pestering the hotel personnel endlessly arguing about hotel policy or the capability of the electrician who was sent to my room, maybe, just maybe, the academic meeting would not have been delayed. The electrical issue in the meeting room would have been resolved earlier.

I had to tell my husband that I had arrived safely. I told him the story about the screwdriver, the hole in the wall, the wires that were pulled out, and the wires connected to my charger. He assured me that I was going to be fine.

Was I fine?

I woke up with hives on my arms, and towards the afternoon, I was literally covered with hives. I was so itchy all over, and I felt feverish. My colleague was able to get medicine, and I felt some relief later in the day. Good thing I packed a coat with me because I had to travel to New Zealand after that. So, I gave my talk while wearing a coat in the grueling heat of summer because some of the hives were still very visible. I must have looked too far out as a speaker on the stage in front of more than five hundred physicians. Feedback was very good, though... I guess the audience was just being kind. I guess I was able to pull it off!

It may be serendipitous that my talk, which should have been at ten in the morning, became six in the evening. I felt better to give a talk in the afternoon rather than that morning because of the hives. One of the reasons why the agenda items were delayed was because of electrical trouble in the meeting room.

Was I to blame because I was being difficult with the hotel receptionist? This led to the delay in the electrician fixing the problem in the meeting room. If

I am not fully to be blamed, maybe at least partly to blame?

I was trying to justify my behavior during that time.

My expectation for a hotel with a high star rating is to have decently dressed employees. My expectation is to have an electrical outlet readily available in the room. My expectation is not to wake up with hives.

Expectations... hotel expectations.

India was not the only country where I had issues concerning hotel rooms. I had one, too, at a popular five-star hotel in the U.S. during one of my business trips.

I must say that hotels, at least in my experience, do listen to customers.

The secret is to speak up to the right person at the right time. And remember that cosmetic injection is pricey, so anything that may add wrinkles to your beautiful face, just let them go!

My style of talking to hotel staff is to first identify the right person, which could be the guest or customer relations personnel, or manager. Otherwise, it may just be a waste of time.

Next, I need to be clear about the situation without any demands or unnecessary emotions so that I will be able to express myself well. This is the difficult part. I need the hotel personnel to not just know but also understand the impact of the situation on me. If I have videos or pictures about an issue at the hotel, this is the time that I show them.

I then ask, what will the hotel do about it?

Let me illustrate a concrete example. I checked into one of the big hotel chains and was awakened by something crawling on my leg. I woke up with small insects, like bed bugs. I immediately took a video of the bugs. I called the hotel receptionist and asked for the hotel manager on duty. I spoke to the hotel manager and stated my predicament. You can just imagine how much emotional control and deep breathing exercises I had to do to be calm in such a situation.

The hotel manager sent a couple of his staff. They removed my clothes and had them immediately dry-cleaned. They helped me pack my things, ensured there was no bug that went along with them, and moved me to the suite room.

Instant room upgrade.

They even gave me a complimentary hotel stay.

I didn't ask to be moved to a suite room or to have a complimentary stay. All I wanted was to have a restful sleep, which I did.

There are ways to solve predicaments in hotels. All you have to do is speak up to the right person at the right time. You may say that with frequent travels and stays in various hotels that I may have achieved a certain status. Yes, I did. And, of course, it helped. That is one of the perks of being a loyal customer.

You may be wondering what happened with my charger connected to the live wires from the hole in the room. I was hesitant to "unplug" it myself, so I asked the hotel guest services for help, and it was handed to me upon checkout.

By the way, the lessons learned and unforgettable experiences involving India did not end there.

CHAPTER FOUR

---※---

Don't Open the Window

India, Part Two

This involved a story that, to this day, sends shivers down my spine every time I think about it. In addition to having your eyebrows and forehead drawn up with your eyes and mouth wide open from the previous chapter, your head will keep on shaking with this story. This story topped it all!

I try to optimize my stay in new places during my travels. I express genuine interest in anything new. I want to learn as much as I can about the culture. I try to learn how a special dish is cooked by talking with the chef and start bussin' about it. I try to learn a new word or two by talking with the hotel staff. I talk to the locals, the waiter, the hotel receptionist, or a store clerk. They always beam with pride when I ask anything about their countries.

Culture. I am impressed with the Canadians for being so polite. My impression is that they have "Sorry" deeply embedded in their vocabulary. I always smile when I talk with my cousins who were born and raised in Canada because they are so respectful and mindful of others around them.

Food. Every time I talk about food, I think of dessert. And every time I think of dessert, I think of *pastel de nata* from Portugal and egg tart from China. Just the thought of a Filipino dessert with preserved fruits and shaved ice or the so-called *halo halo* makes my eyes twinkle. I heard that it is a favorite of Vanessa Hudgens as well. No surprise there since her mom is originally from the Philippines.

Usual pleasantries that I learned from those travels always make me smile. Learning another language for me is a good exercise for the brain. Words such as *Hogy Vagy* in Hungarian, which means "How are you?" or *Shalom* in Jewish, which means "Hello, goodbye and peace."

Countries in Asia are usually hospitable and customer-focused. Some countries on other continents are also very welcoming to foreigners. Switzerland is a country like Japan where I felt safe. I always love to travel and talk to people from the Nordic countries because they are always smiling when you talk to them. Think about the countries ranked among the highest when it comes to the happiness index.[3] Yes—happy, and content faces everywhere.

There are so many unforgettable and great experiences as well that made me want to return to many countries and this time for a vacation. From the *Jardin Exotique* in Monaco to the Mayan temple ruins of Mexico, to the Table Mountain in South Africa, to the predawn darkness of Mount Batur in Indonesia—everything is so breathtaking. Of course, the tallest buildings, such as the Petronas towers in Malaysia and Taipei 101, are truly phenomenal. These and many more incredible experiences made me understand other people's cultures, behaviors, and perspectives. In the process, I also made awesome friends from various countries.

So back to India.

I had a couple of hours of spare time before my next meeting, so I figured I had enough time to explore the place. It was the time of *Kumbha Mela*, so I just wanted to catch a glimpse of the ritual dip into the Ganges and Yamuna rivers. I wanted to get my mind off things as I was heavily working and didn't have a good night's sleep the day before. I didn't bother to touch the delicious meal served during the flight or even taste the beautifully crafted food by a famous chef at the airport lounge. I was already adding on weight, neglecting my daily exercises, and mindlessly eating when stressed.

---

[3] https://worldpopulationreview.com/country-rankings/happiest-countries-in-the-world

The hotel clerk was able to fulfill my request to watch the ritual with one exception—the driver couldn't speak English. The hotel clerk patiently explained to the driver what I wanted to do. During the tour, I was told to stay put in the car, which I promised. Streets were crowded, and it was not safe to wander around.

It was hot inside the car, and gosh, what was that smell? The driver mumbled something—I guess he mentioned that the car's air conditioner was broken, or the car was not cleaned properly. You can just imagine the headache because of the heat, sweat all over my body, and my hand covering my mouth and nose. The torment was so hard to handle while inside the car.

Wherever the driver went, there were so many cows and people.

We were caught in a traffic jam for like eternity, and I decided to do something about my predicament. I already had cold, clammy sweats. I needed to breathe in the fresh air. I opened my car window for just a bit. The driver mumbled something, which I interpreted as I could open it fully. That was one of the biggest mistakes of my life.

I learned later on that what he actually said was, "Don't open the window!"

Talk about lost in translation.

The next series of events was totally unforeseen.

Suddenly, there was a frail baby girl on my lap thrown from outside the car window. The baby was wrapped in a shabby and dirty blanket, dark-skinned with a *hindi* or a red dot on her forehead. She was crying the whole time. I assumed the baby was just a month old and, if older, was extremely malnourished.

I didn't touch her at all since I was still quietly suffering from hysteria. And yes, there is such a thing as quiet hysteria for me. It is when I am overpowered with so much unexplained emotion so strong that I can barely utter a word. Heart pounding, muscles stiff, ashen pale... you get the picture.

Then a woman wearing tattered clothes was screaming something outside the car window. I did not have any clue what she was saying. Was she the mother? Was she asking for money in exchange for her child? Was this a way to beg for alms? And that was for me to get the chance to hold an Indian baby and pay? Or pay her because she gave me her baby? She was crying and seemingly pleading the entire time.

I was very afraid and held my purse tightly. I was incredibly worried that it might be snatched away at any moment from me. The baby was still crying the entire time while slowly moving her arms and legs. I did not even vibe or do anything at all to pacify the baby's incessant crying.

The driver was yelling at the woman from his seat. I thought that he might be driving the woman away. And with a very annoyed look, he got off from the car and started shouting at the woman. The woman was pointing at me the entire time. Then the driver opened my door and got hold of the baby, angrily kicked the door shut, and handed the baby back to her. The woman did not want to get the baby and was about to leave. The driver got hold of her hand and forced the baby back to her. The baby was incessantly crying during the entire time. The driver was lashing back at her, and they had an exchange of words that I had never understood. It sounded like they were fighting; the woman was already wailing and was pointing at the baby and me. The driver was pointing at the baby and her.

My pulse was racing, and my whole body trembled, not because of the heat or obnoxious smell but because of what I had just witnessed. I stared at my lap where the baby had previously landed and extended my arms forward as if expecting it may happen again or maybe imagining that I was holding the baby.

The driver went back to the car and looked so upset. He honked at other cars and moved his way out of the traffic jam while shouting at other pedestrians and drivers. He went back to the hotel and spoke to the hotel receptionist. I guess he was explaining why we had to return earlier and that he was not able to fulfill his obligations to drive me where I wanted to go.

I spoke to the hotel receptionist and asked him to let the driver tell the entire story of what had just happened.

After they spoke, the hotel receptionist narrated the story.

The woman who threw the baby at my lap was indeed the mother. That baby was her seventh. The family was living in a house made of scraps of construction materials with bare soil as their flooring. Their space was so small that they had to take turns lying down on the ground to sleep. Both the woman and her husband did not have any work, and they relied on scrap food thrown at them on the streets or whatever they could get from trash bins.

When the woman saw me, an idea crossed her mind. If she gave me her baby, even though I was a complete stranger to her, she felt that her baby would live a good life and would have a better future. Her baby would have a chance to be free from their miserable situation. One of her children just passed away due to hunger the day before that, and she did not want her baby to experience the same fate as well. She did not ask for money. She pleaded for me to take care of her baby.

While I was still horrified by the event that just happened inside the car, I began to examine my behavior involving that instance.

Was the mother right that I would be able to give that baby a chance for a better future? Of course.

How would I be able to take her with me out of India? I arrived alone yet would leave with another human being. I could ask colleagues or friends about the process, so maybe that problem could be resolved.

How would I explain myself to my family? I already have three sons. I guess they would be ecstatic to have a new baby girl in the family.

To this day, I always ask myself the following questions. How is the baby now? Did she turn out as a beggar like the rest of her family? Was she given to another mother? And the saddest part that I cannot take off my mind is this—is she still alive?

Until now, there is that lingering feeling of guilt every time I see women on the streets asking for alms while holding babies.

Why did I even think the mother would snatch away my purse?

What if I just took the baby and ran off? What if I just brought the baby back with me?

Did I ever hate the mother because of her decision? For some reason, I did not. She is a mother like me. In fact, that situation awakened my responsibility as a mother.

There was some point in my life when I prioritized work over my family. I guess this applies not only to the expats but also to some of you who tried to juggle work and family at the same time. I guess it was more pronounced for an expat like me. Maybe because I always think so much money was spent every time just for me to relocate to another country. Hence, I feel indebted, and in my own way, I need to pay it back.

You may not believe it, but work came ahead of my sick child at one point.

There was one time when I needed to travel to Austria for a business meeting. The departure time of my flight was late at night.

My youngest son, who was five years old then, was sick during that time. And, of course, when a child is sick, the child always clings to Mommy. Same for him; he kept on asking for me and wanted me to be by his side the entire time.

But I had to go.

When I told him about it, he gathered all his strength and pointed at the window. He said that it was so dark that the pilot would not be able to see where we would be going. He made excuses and reasons just for me not to leave his side. He kept on begging for me to stay.

He also said that I should not leave him because it was my responsibility to take care of him. He said that was a mommy's responsibility, not a daddy's responsibility. I felt a dagger just pierced through my heart, and my face was covered with a river of tears. My husband brought him inside his room. In between sobs, my son kept on calling my name, pleading for me not to leave. I stood there silent while staring at my laptop until I couldn't hear him anymore... until his voice became muffled behind closed doors.

With a heavy heart, I had to leave. I kept on calling my son on my way to the airport, at the lounge, and prior to boarding. But he was so tired from crying that he was already asleep. I kept on crying on the way to the airport, at the lounge, and during the flight. The flight attendant and chief purser approached me several times, asking if I was okay during the flight. I guess as a million miler, I got a lot of attention. I had to apply a lot of eye makeup to conceal the puffiness.

My husband tended to him while I was away.

I kept on praying fervently that what he had was just a self-limiting viral infection. That he would be fine. He would get over it. He would not remember that his mommy left him behind and prioritized her work.

You can just imagine how I overcompensated for the lost time when I returned.

Good thing he was cheerful and was back to his usual self when I returned home. Most importantly, he did not hate me. Not sure if the toy that I bought from the Czech Republic did the trick.

I developed a feeling of inferiority as a mother because I ended up comparing myself with the mother from India. She epitomized the essence of a mother. She prioritized the welfare of her baby.

Did I hate the poverty she was in that might have pushed her to give away her baby? Perhaps. Poverty was so pronounced that it is the only reason I can think of involving that situation. Coming from the Philippines, where poverty and social stratification are evident, whereby the rich have so many privileges, and the poor have daily struggles, I can easily relate to India.

Ahh... The Philippines. It is a beautiful country, with rich biodiversity and spectacular beaches. The country is also laden with poverty. There are slum areas and many beggars in the streets as well, especially in Manila. So much productive time is also lost due to traffic and pedestrians being all over the place. There are so many people there as well. I used to rebuff a beggar who pleaded outside my car window during heavy traffic when I was still living in the Philippines. That flashback added to my guilt.

I was also trying to rationalize why I held my purse firmly instead of the baby while inside the car. Of course, growing up in the Philippines, in the back of my mind, I always think that any situation, whether unusual or ordinary, may lead to a certain crime happening. Somebody may just stop you and pretend to ask for directions, and suddenly your purse will be snatched.

What I learned from that experience in India was not to judge others easily. There... a life lesson revealed. We need to really understand what others need rather than assume what those needs are.

I learned the value of listening. Well, in that instance, this was a challenge because of the language difficulty. But at any rate, without any language barrier, I should really listen.

I learned from the Indian mother that no matter what, my family should come first. I should always consider the welfare of my family ahead of anything else.

I also realized that I am blessed. That time while in India, I was complaining about not having a good night's sleep because I was so stressed, when in fact, I had a very comfortable bed to sleep on. I did not eat because I wanted to go on a diet despite the delicious food served in front of me.

I learned the fact that I should be grateful and thankful for what I have. And that I should share my blessings and do more charity work.

One of the famous quotes of Mother Theresa goes like this, "We cannot do great things, only small things with great love." If we start by doing small things to help others, perhaps in some way, we may be able to make a difference in somebody else's life. Perhaps we may be able to help a mother and a baby, like the situation in India.

After that event, my husband and I became more committed to doing volunteer medical missions to the depressed communities in the Philippines every time we get the chance. We did those in collaboration with the Catholic church or the Philippine consulate.

It is always rewarding to put a smile on somebody else's face because we helped them with their illness. I remember receiving notes from people my husband and I helped in the past. In their own little way, they expressed how grateful they were. We even had our sons donate their old toys. They saved money from their school allowance to buy school backpacks to be given away to needy schoolchildren. They have been assisting us with our medical missions and our feeding programs.

That feeling of happiness that engulfs us each time we do our charity work is so exhilarating that no amount of a relocation package can beat it. No amount of wealth in this world can top that feeling. Nobody would dare say, "This ain't it, chief." We were so committed that nothing stopped us even after I contracted dengue fever during one of our medical missions.

The value of charity work can never be disputed.

The COVID-19 pandemic put a halt to our charity work. We needed be more creative. We ended up conducting telemedical missions to those who needed medical advice on COVID-19 prevention and home treatment. The pandemic also made me reexamine my priorities again. So much so that I regretted the time when I responded to a business call while on vacation instead of spending precious time with my dad. I did not know then that it was the last time that I would ever see my dad alive because of travel restrictions during the pandemic. I should have dedicated every minute to him. I can never bring that back.

We often did our charity medical missions in my dad's rural hometown. I always wore a smile on my face and walked into the venues with so much energy when I treat the patients. In those medical missions, my happiness and fulfillment came from two sources. First, from the pride I gave my dad for being a physician because he worked so hard to send me to medical school. Second, from the inner feeling of bliss for being able to help others.

However, due to safety reasons, we had to close the venues at five o'clock in the afternoon.

The importance of five o'clock p.m.

CHAPTER FIVE

---※---

It's Five P.M.

Japan, Part One

Five o'clock in the afternoon always sticks in my mind every time I think of Japan. It was not because of the experience upon arrival that I will mention next... it was more than that.

My first travel to Japan was very memorable. Upon arrival, it was not just the usual immigration and baggage claim. It included meeting Japanese men wearing suits who didn't speak English. With the use of sign language, I was told to sign a document, but I was clueless about its contents because it was all written in Japanese. I had to sign it as soon as possible so they could have enough time to submit such a document, as it was almost five o'clock in the afternoon.

There you go, the first five o'clock p.m. memory involving Japan.

The excitement involving my first travel to Japan was replaced by fear since Filipino women during that time were known to work as entertainers, or *Japayuki* in slang, a term that was derogatory and frowned upon. It was the same word used by the immigration officer in the Philippines when I got held up at the airport. *Japayuki* is like "lady of the night," so to speak. The story goes that they were asked to sign documents they didn't understand upon arrival in Japan, and then they were transferred to bars or nightclubs where they should start to work. Hence, that "welcome party" involving the Japanese men in suits asking me to sign a document made me shiver all over. What would happen to me? What would happen after I signed?

Speaking of *Japayuki*, which is becoming less and less nowadays, I met several of them while in Japan. Most of the time, the reason why they end up as *Japayuki* is that they are financially helping their family members back home.

In my opinion, this is not a good part of Filipino culture. Filipino families take pride in having a family member outside of the Philippines. Families back home in the Philippines have a certain expectation of being financially supported by a family member based overseas. Overseas Filipino workers sacrifice a lot toiling in a foreign land. They live hundreds or even thousands of miles away from home to support their families in the Philippines. They live away from their husbands or wives, away from their children, and away from their families.

This is a controversial topic that I had discussions about with my close friends who are based overseas. It is always pricey to return home because of such expectations. I remember one episode of Suze Orman's show regarding a Filipino sending money to the Philippines. She did mention during that time that it is a Filipino culture and is very challenging to change. Filipinos who are working overseas think of their families back home sometimes more than their own welfare while working in a foreign country. The movie "Hello, Love, Goodbye" which starred Kathryn Bernardo and Alden Richards depicted such struggles. In fact, there are roughly two million overseas Filipino workers. The Philippine population is one hundred fifteen million.[4] Do the math.

Hence, overseas Filipino workers are called local heroes because they help the Philippine economy and, more importantly, their families. There are many who work in the middle east as contract workers, domestic helpers in Hong Kong and Singapore, caregivers in Europe, and healthcare professionals in the U.S. These are just some examples of local heroes. The *Japayuki* should not be excluded from that list, despite a seemingly degrading job that they ended up with. That term is

---

[4] https://psa.gov.ph/statistics/survey/labor-and-employment/survey-overseas-filipinos#:~:text=The%20number%20of%20Overseas%20Filipinos,2.18%20million%20reported%20in%202019.&text=The%20number%20of%20Overseas%20Contract,from%202.11%20million%20in%202019

rarely used recently, since entertainer's visa became limited and Filipinos coming to Japan are increasingly highly skilled. I hope that the image of Filipinos in Japan is becoming better. I hope it will evolve into something like the image of Filipinos in the U.S., that of being educated and professional. Most importantly, I hope that overseas Filipino workers, regardless of their work, will be respected by other Filipinos and other nationalities.

Back to the story ...

There are times when I want things to be rushed or finished quickly. So maybe that was the reason I did not bother to read the information at all. If I had read my welcome packet prior to departure or even on the plane, I would have remained excited, and my hands would not have trembled while signing the document. I should have known that the "welcome party" or the men in suits were there to document my arrival to the Japanese government and hand me my landing allowance (Yay!).

There you go. Another lesson revealed. Take the time to understand what you are getting yourself into and do not be derailed from knowing vital information by too much excitement.

I would like to tell you upfront that I do love Japan. I gave birth to our third son there, I learned another language, and I learned to live a healthy lifestyle because of the good food and walks at the parks along beautifully curated Japanese gardens. I guess, more importantly, I made a lot of friends.

Japan is very advanced, so beautiful, and clean. People are so honest and respectful. It is very rich in culture, and its history is magnificent. I first came to Japan to pursue higher education and further my career in the 1990s. Despite the stories that my grandmother told me about the war, I love the country and its people. I always wanted to return. And I did return. I returned as an accomplished career woman and worked as an executive.

Japan changed me. I was transformed to be less spiteful. To be more kind and accepting. To just be content with anything. "It is what it is" is a useful statement that always plays inside my head, and I got to use that phrase more often while in Japan and even after leaving the country.

But of course, there is no such thing as perfect.

There was a time when I was reproached because I hugged my sons in public. People glared at my husband and me when we held hands while walking in the park or spoke loudly, or talked to each other while on the train. We felt alienated because we did not behave as others would have expected. We even overheard comments that we were behaving in a certain way because we were not like them. Come to think of it, the residency card during that time was labeled "Alien Registration Card," so boom... Aliens, welcome (or not welcome) to Japan.

My two older sons were first enrolled at a local public school with a good number of foreign students. One day, the principal informed me that wristwatches were not allowed in school, as it was not in harmony with other kids in school. So goodbye robot-faced watches. My sons needed to wear the same length of socks and the same school items. Every day, they dragged their feet to go to school because they felt they were losing their identities. It was a blessing that we found a way to transfer them to an international school.

Norms and standards ...

Now comes the second story about five o'clock p.m.

While in Japan, there were several instances when I needed to submit a report at the administration office during a specified period.

One time, I arrived at the office a couple of minutes past the hour of five in the afternoon. Everyone was still there. I thought that because they were still there that they would still accept my report.

Unfortunately, my report was not accepted because it was past five o'clock p.m.

Seriously? It was only a couple of minutes! I did not blurt out these loudly, of course. That was another thing I learned. I was able to control my emotions (I think).

The office lady explained that the requirement clearly stated the deadline, and since I missed it, I must wait for the next round of the submission timeline. That meant I would not be able to take another course requirement, and I needed to do double time to fulfill all the requirements together in the next semester. She said that she was only doing her job and was executing the rule because that was expected of her, and that was the norm.

She was correct.

It was my fault that I was late and not hers. She could have accepted, but no, she didn't. It was because she was doing her job. That was normal for her.

Speaking of normal ...

There was one incident that a bullet train or *shinkansen* that I boarded suddenly stopped in between stations because of a severe thunderstorm. That bullet train stopped in a tunnel. It was so dark, and I only heard the announcements about the reason why the train stopped, where we were located, and that we should remain seated and calm.

One would expect people to be standing from their seats or talking or making calls, contacting their families. But no, it was so quiet. If that had happened in other countries, there might have been at least some noise among the passengers. But as I gazed at my seatmate and those across me, they just had their eyes closed.

Were they asleep?

Were they praying?

Or were they just behaving like that because it was the norm? The norm was for them to close their eyes and not move or panic despite the situation while inside the train. Come to think of it, many passengers inside the train close their eyes anyway.

I guess they are just used to these kinds of situations that, for them, they trust that it will pass and that we will ultimately arrive at our destination.

Was it because they practice patience a lot? My observation about Japan is that most Japanese are very patient. They have festivals to appreciate the cherry blossoms and patiently wait for fireworks. They always patiently fall in line. They don't get bored gazing at the rocks at the rock garden in Kyoto, and they just sit down and observe the beauty of nature.

Getting used to not panicking when a bullet train stops in the middle of nowhere was a norm.

Patiently waiting for their turn was the norm.

Or the culture.

Being patient, in general, is one of their virtues. Being disciplined is also one of their virtues. Japan is the country where I learned the virtue of discipline and the value of being patient.

With any relocation or travel, you get to absorb something good. You get to learn something new. That's part of it. An essential part of it. Another life lesson revealed.

The idea of being patient may not always be advantageous. As mentioned, I gave birth to our third son in Japan, and I experienced so much pain post-cesarean section. I requested for pain reliever, but because it was not time yet for my next dose, I was told to be patient. *Gaman shitte kudasai* or "Please be patient."

Tolerate it. In other words... "Suck it up!" In my clinical practice, as much as possible, I never want my patients to experience pain. Could that be one of the reasons why the birth rate in Japan is so low? Because women had to tolerate the pain? Is that okay because it is acceptable?

Would it be okay for the office lady to be flexible and accept my report? Perhaps, but that may have negated the rule in place regarding the submission of reports. Rules are there to be followed. I needed to be disciplined and observe the rule. If she had accepted my report, she might have been disproved by her co-workers because that was not the norm.

What about the unique individuality of each and every person? The experience my sons had at a Japanese school was a huge hurdle for them. If it was acceptable for a Japanese to just close their eyes and not panic, would it not be acceptable for an emotional or demonstrative foreigner to react or display affection to her children or spouse?

As a foreigner in Japan, the norm or expectation is already different, maybe to a certain degree. There are times when, as a foreigner, I can get away with some things. Like maybe crossing the street in a hurry with no cars passing by even if the sign says, "Do not walk." But not in a way that others may consider disturbing or even not conforming to their standards, like what the principal told me regarding the wristwatches of my sons.

Learning the life of a foreigner includes learning to belong in an extraordinarily unusual environment. Learning to belong means learning the language, history, and culture in order to understand them. Learning to understand means accepting the things that are social norms and societal expectations. Another life lesson revealed.

Apart from being transformed to be less mean, become less bitchy ...

However ...

During my initial stay in Japan, I also lost my voice. Being a woman made me lose my voice. I learned how to be quiet, to be in a corner, and let the men lead the way. Being a woman in that country meant not being offered a seat or being opened a door. Being a woman in that country meant not being given an opportunity to be front and center, as a woman needed to take a back seat. I felt at one point that being a woman and a foreigner also meant losing one's identity.

Would you believe that I used to bow and talk in a high pitch when I spoke to somebody on the telephone? I used to cover my mouth when I laughed, and my laughter was very much inhibited way back then. That was not me. That was a different Jovelle.

As a foreigner, there is already that element that you are considered an outsider in Japan.

As a woman, there is that additional hurdle of a patriarchal society that was vividly intoxicating when I was there.

Let me tell you more about it in the next chapter.

CHAPTER SIX

The Cable TV Subscription

Japan, Part Two

Being in a male-dominated society is tough. Even in the field of medicine, it was a challenge. My specialty, Obstetrics and Gynecology, has at least more than a handful, if not dominated by women specialists in several countries. In Japan, that is the opposite.

Some Japanese female physicians had to leave work after marriage because the expectation of society for a wife is for her to tend to her husband, become pregnant, raise the kids, and take care of the family. Hence, most of them cannot pursue their careers anymore.

The role of Japanese women in society...

Women give chocolates to men during Valentine's Day. Men are the ones wooed rather than women. It was unusual for a man to make the first move during courtship, and it is usually the woman who takes the initiative. Wives receiving flowers from their husbands are extraordinarily rare.

I had observed during that time that wives are expected to prepare and cook food for their husbands every time. Wives are also expected to prepare the bathtub or so-called *o-furo* for their husbands. Apparently, conversations rarely happen inside the Japanese household. Usual conversations in households are "*Tadaima*" in Japanese, which means "I am home," "*Gohan*," which means "prepare food" in this context, and "*Itadakimasu*," which means "I will eat." Sometimes, the wife does not eat together with the husband if there are visitors. I sometimes prepare and cook food for my husband when I get the chance, though he cooks more than I do because he is a better cook than I am. I do not think I ever prepared his bath. We spend so much time together, whether doing a hobby or sharing a lot of stories while eating. If we have visitors at home, both my husband and I eat jointly with them.

I must say that the most tolerant human beings in this world are the Japanese wives, hands down. There is a saying that the best wives are the Japanese. Traditional Japanese wives are known to be submissive and faithful to their husbands. They are known to take the time to care for their children. Their sweet voice, composure, and politeness make them a better option.

One time, one of my friends asked me for help. She wanted me to talk to her husband so I could convince him to subscribe to cable TV so she could learn English. Apparently, she informed her husband about it, but her request was not granted. The husband also happens to be a friend.

I was reluctant at first because I thought that I might be invading a husband-wife relationship. Especially since both of them are my friends. So why not? Why not help a friend in need, in this case, the wife?

Not sure if I have better negotiation skills than the wife, but I guess I must have had. I may have developed that skill at home. I always have lively discussions with my husband and sons and may have taught my sons to express their opinions well. Especially with Justin, my second, who is highly skilled in negotiations and challenges everything that I say, so I learned to be evidence-based. I cannot use the phrase, "Because I said so," to any of them since they know that such a response is not good enough. I must have taught them well to speak out because it will take a lot of convincing why I have to say "Yes" or "No." I end up using "We will see" just to stop the conversation and move on or as an excuse just so it will make them feel that I will look into their requests without necessarily overpromising.

I guess in the process of having several encounters with my Japanese female friends, I may have taught them not to be afraid to voice out their opinions and not bite their tongues. I may have trained them, in my own little way, to have honest conversations with their husbands. I may have taught them to express what they really feel and not be afraid to mention what they really need.

That is why foreplay is important in a relationship, which I will describe in detail in the last chapter.

The next time I met with the wife, she was delighted and also practiced English with me. Her husband agreed to a cable TV subscription so she could watch English programs and learn in the process. She was very grateful for it. I hinted that it was her own doing and not mine, and that I merely provided further information on why it needed to be done. She was beaming with pride because it was her first accomplishment as a wife to have her request granted by the husband exclusively for her use. I was so happy with the idea that I was able to help somebody not take the back seat and be the driver instead. I was able to make her realize that societal expectation does not need to be applied all the time.

I told her she could be powerful if she wanted to be.

Well, come to think of it. She could have easily purchased the cable subscription herself since she has her husband's bank card, and the husband only relies on the allowance she gives him. That is not uncommon in Japan. Because the wives take care of all the needs of the family, they manage the finances of the household. If you possess the money, shouldn't you have the power?

Maybe not powerful enough to make decisions. Even as minor as a cable TV subscription?

Wives in Japan have different fates in their marriages.

Some of the wives accept their roles to serve the husband, raise the children, set aside their careers if there is one, and become economically dependent on the husbands. They may get used to such a life. Other wives may realize that they need to have a career, and some may have more conversations with their husbands. Some of them end up in divorce. If both the husband

and the wife agree to the divorce, a decision can be issued for the divorce to happen in two weeks.

These situations are not unique to Japanese wives. Similar situations can be found elsewhere, too.

I have also seen husbands suffer from divorce. For example, there are large financial settlements that need to be made. I came across someone who had to leave his current job and accept another one because of a huge sign-on bonus. When asked further, he needed the money to pay alimony because of a recent divorce.

Not all situations are the same. I am not saying that women or wives are heroes here. I am also not saying that men or husbands are to blame. A relationship needs a lot of nurturing, love, and sacrifice. It takes a lot of patience to solidify such a relationship.

A torn relationship has an impact not just on both parties involved but also on their children, if they have any. A broken home also has an impact on the people around them.

There are a lot of famous songs involving broken relationships that give us a sense of the impact on the affected family and others around them. The song by Bruno Mars, "When I Was Your Man," depicts a picture from a man's perspective. Adele's song, "Someone Like You," is reflective of the feelings of a woman as well. Pink's song "Family Portrait" depicted her experiences as a child of divorce parents.

Some individuals who are expatriated also leave their families behind. Expatriation or relocation, or distance can also break relationships. But what about the saying, "Absence makes the heart grow fonder?"

Perhaps, to a certain degree, absence does make the heart grow fonder. Yet I have seen children not appropriately cared for and ultimately steered towards the wrong path in life. I have seen spouses having extra-marital relationships all because the other partner or a parent is far away.

I chose to be with my family and took them with me wherever I got expatriated. That is always part of the package. And because we were together, we were able to overcome the challenges together. And because we were together, we were able to nurture our relationship and become closer to each other. And because we were together, we share common stories that we always relieve.

I guess that is the greatest satisfaction about relocation and travel—being with your loved ones.

As an obstetrician-gynecologist, obviously, my patients are women. Sometimes, their partners or husbands join during consultations. Occasionally, I am asked for guidance about conflicts in their married lives ranging from how they can sexually satisfy each other to managing their emotions. How should they communicate with their partner? As far as communication is concerned, the last chapter of this book involving The Foreplay can be useful.

Oftentimes, there are pressures from other family members or society that interfere with the couple's decisions involving their relationships. Those pressures force the couple to be in a relationship. On the other hand, those pressures may also drive away one of the partners from a relationship.

Speaking of the pressure of society …

CHAPTER SEVEN

Sumo

Japan, Part Three

Indulge me as I continue to talk about Japan since a good chunk of my life was spent living there.

For those of you who may not be familiar with sumo, it is Japanese-style wrestling. In fact, it is the national sport of Japan and is done with a religious ritual, exemplified by the purification of the sumo ring with salt. Such purity also meant that women are banned from participating in any sumo tournament or sumo ceremony. Women cannot even touch or step on the ring.

Does that mean that women are contaminants or inappropriate in a *dohyo* or sumo ring? They say that we women are unclean because of our monthly period of menstruation and bleeding associated with childbirth.

There was one time when an elderly male mayor collapsed while giving a speech at a sumo event. Few women rushed to the ring to give emergency treatment. You would expect that in such a situation, which may be life-threatening, saving the life should be the priority. But you know what? An announcement was made that the women should leave the sumo ring immediately. Women were ordered to leave the ring due to rules banning females from going to that sacred space. The women were repeatedly told to step away from the sumo arena.

There was one time when a governor of a city, who happened to be a woman, was forced to present the prize to the sumo champion outside of the ring. She presented the prize on a walkway next to the ring, despite her requests to be allowed to enter, given her political authority.

As a foreigner, you need to learn to understand why certain actions are done in a certain way and why certain behaviors are such. Sometimes, you end up sucking it up, or sometimes you just shake your head in disbelief. Other times, you may challenge it. Why not? Especially if it does not conform to acceptable behavior in your mind.

So, what is acceptable behavior? Is it acceptable not to allow women to enter a sacred place of a religious tournament to help a person who needs medical attention? Is it acceptable not to allow a high-ranking official to enter the sumo ring because she is a woman?

In this modern day and age, the plight of women in Japan is something that until now remains an enigma. In fact, Japan ranks 120th among the 156 countries when it comes to gender gap ranking in 2021.[5] According to the World Economic Forum, women's participation in the political and economic areas remain low in Japan. The country did close its gender gap in primary education. The other G-7 countries ranked between eleven to thirty. In Asia, the Philippines is the best-performing country at number seventeen.

A sad reality involving Japan's gender gap emerged again into the spotlight due to sexist remarks made by a former prime minister. He was forced to step down as head of the 2020 Paralympic and Olympic Committees. He alluded to the fact that meetings with women tend to "drag" because women talk too much.

Do women really talk too much in meetings? I talk in meetings, but I do not think it is too much. I do talk to provide a productive contribution to the topic and not just for the sake of talking. I keep quiet if I do not know. I will share more stories about my experience in the workplace, specifically in the corporate world. I will share those stories in Chapter Nine. By the way, the title of that chapter is "She Won't Last Long."

My opinion, since I have lived in Japan for a long time, is that the situation of women in Japan remains an area that needs special attention. It is not just a tick in the box to have more women in the workplace. It is

---

[5] https://www.weforum.org/reports/global-gender-gap-report-2022/digest/#:~:text=North%20America%20leads%20all%20regions,72.6%25%20of%20its%20gender%20gap

not just a superficial metric to provide maternity leave. Will it be better if there is provision of training and education for women? What about hiring or promoting them ahead of men? I believe it is beyond those. It is deeply rooted in the fundamental element of changing the mindset. It is not just a superficial checklist to flaunt and for the rest of the world to acknowledge.

There are a lot of initiatives that do try to minimize the gender gap. While those are evident, and several companies have various strategies in place to encourage the hiring and career growth of women, there remains that norm or societal expectation about what women's role in society should be. Initiatives are there to help enable women to take care of their families while being productive at work. Are those enough?

There are also several initiatives that tackle women's empowerment. The United Nations had goals related to women's access to education and other opportunities, such as work. The U.S. empowered women by passing laws and inclusion of women in politics providing social acceptance of women in power.

In general, there is still some improvement that must be made; perhaps the predicament of women is more extreme in different cultures compared with others. In fact, even if fictional in nature, one of the episodes of the Korean TV drama series "Extraordinary Attorney Woo" took into account the condition of women in the workplace. There was an episode where married women were asked to resign from work to take care of their families, support their husbands, and let their husbands work.

So, what should be the societal expectation? Is it something that becomes a rule that should not be broken?

A well-known societal expectation in the field of medicine is that one should not be an attending physician in situations when the objectivity may be lost. It may be true, but what if it is a life-threatening situation such as the sumo event I described earlier?

The last baby I delivered was the most memorable obstetrical procedure I ever did. This was when I was still active in my surgical practice. The field of obstetrics and gynecology entails quick decision-making skillset while exercising utmost care. The mind has to be clear, the hands have to be steady, and the emotion needs to be controlled.

The delivery of that baby was a complicated case. It involved a mother who was having early labor pains and high blood pressure. The early labor pains until seven months of pregnancy was previously controlled. However, in the middle of the night, I had to attend to this patient because she was then having severe labor pains. She was exhibiting symptoms that her uterus was about to rupture. Her blood pressure continued to shoot up. And to make matters worse, I was not able to hear the heartbeat of the baby.

We rushed to the hospital to do further evaluation. The condition warranted emergency cesarean section. The resident physicians who are in-training were the only ones in the hospital during that unholy hour. This case was complicated to manage, and this is one of the cases that obstetricians are most afraid of. Making the decision quickly to do emergency surgery was the easy part; the difficult one was deciding who would perform it.

I had doubts in my head, not related to whether I was capable of doing the surgery but whether I was the right person to do it. I was so exhausted and was not able to sleep the day before because of a difficult gynecological procedure that I had to perform. This was a life-saving procedure for the mother and child.

The mother of the baby told me, "You can do this. I know you can!"

With some hesitation, as if I was walking barefoot on a flaming coal, I did not want to, but I had to perform the urgent emergency cesarean section.

I locked eyes with the anesthesiologist. He nodded. Suddenly, there was an enigmatic force that steered me towards doing a familiar task that I had performed countless times. As if I was just given a miraculous drug that gave me full control of all my faculties, I started to perform the surgery. My hands were not shaking, my mind was alert. I called out and used appropriate instruments with so much confidence—knife, clamp, scissors, sponge, retractor. After a couple of minutes, a very tiny baby boy was born, just enough for both of my open hands to hold. I had to pump his chest with my pinky finger because he was not breathing. Oh... my God! Was I too late? I was crying with joy when the tiny baby gasped. One of his tiny hands made a weak grip on my pinky finger as if telling me to stop reviving him because he is going to be fine. I handed him over to the neonatologist (pediatrician specializing in premature babies) for further care.

Funny, I called out a sponge to control the bleeding of the operative field, but instead of handing me the sponge, the nurse wiped my face because it was full of tears. She smiled at me, giving me the assurance that the worst was over. Of course, I was still worried about the mother. Good thing that the operation and her condition after the delivery of the baby were uneventful, despite signs of complications due to high blood pressure during pregnancy.

The baby had no anatomical defects but because of his extreme prematurity, he had a low chance of survival. He stayed inside the incubator for a long time. He is a fighter because he survived! He is the smallest and youngest baby to ever survive in that hospital during that time.

Both mother and baby are well.

Oh, did I tell you that the baby I delivered is my nephew, the firstborn son in that family, and the mother is my sister?

Can you imagine the emotion I was in during that time? I was drowning in a sea of uncertainty and plunged into a realm of darkness, yet I needed to have steady hands and was expected to know what to do and how to proceed. I needed to objectively determine what instruments to call out and what medications to be administered while managing my emotions at the same time. What if my decision to do the surgery was wrong? What if I was late? What if there were complications during and after the surgery? What if the baby died?

What if the mother died? If something wrong happened, I would never be able to forgive myself.

But I had to make that difficult decision.

The norm or standard or societal expectation is not the rule. Oftentimes, we need to make hard decisions. It may not be of the same magnitude as my own experience involving the last baby I delivered. But when we are confronted with life-threatening situations, societal expectation is put to the test, and the well-being of others becomes the priority.

The delivery of my nephew, Niko, defied that norm. My sister, Jing, was so composed during that time and trusted me wholeheartedly. She defied that norm, too.

Good thing that the elderly mayor who collapsed inside the sumo ring did not have a life-threatening condition and he survived. Good thing that the Japan Sumo Association apologized to the women who tried to revive him.

We can defy a norm or standard as long as it does not compromise somebody else's safety and, in fact, can save somebody else's life.

We need to trust others who defy that norm because it may lead to a better outcome. That is what my sister did.

But there are situations where we may feel helpless because we cannot do anything. It is either we are not allowed to do so, such as what happened with the sumo tournament, or we are too affected by societal norms and expectations.

It is up to you.

If it is not a life-threatening situation, and if you decide not to do anything, my response to that is, "It is what it is!" I know some people hate that phrase. But, "It is what it is!"

CHAPTER EIGHT

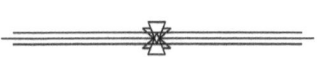

The Lift

Singapore

Again, speaking of norms and standards.

I will not go through a long list of things that are prohibited in Singapore, such as chewing gum. There are laws with corresponding penalties involving certain behaviors that may be considered acceptable in another country but not in Singapore. I am sure there is an explanation for why such laws are in place. Combing through those things is not the intent of this chapter.

Singapore is clean and advanced. I loved the Marina Bay Sands and the Night Safari. Food is so delectable like the *hokkien* and the *bak kut teh*. My favorite cocktail is the Singapore sling, and I always plunge into an open bar party with it. JK (just kidding). I do not drink anything alcoholic and barely sip even in a social context.

We relocated to Singapore and stayed there for almost three years. We had the privilege of living in a private condominium in an English-speaking country with a low crime rate. Finally, we got relocated to an Asian country where we understood and could relate better. Yes! There are many expats in Singapore. There are many foreigners in Singapore.

One of the things we were asked when we first arrived was whether we would hire a domestic helper. Domestic helpers or maids are common in Singapore. In fact, as of 2019 statistics, one in five Singapore households employed a maid.[6] Maids are there to do general housework and look after the elderly, young children, or family members with disabilities.

I had a chance to encounter many maids from the Philippines since a third out of all the 240,000 maids in Singapore are from the Philippines. I will not go through the depressing stories about maids being maltreated or abused, whether emotionally or physically, whether reported in the news or not. We should not forget that there are good stories of maids in Singapore as well. Some of them become an extended family of their employers. Not to mention the economic advantage.

---

[6] https://www.statista.com/statistics/953137/singapore-foreign-domestic-workers-employed/#:~:text=Number%20of%20foreign%20domestic%20workers%20%20Singapore%202013%2D2021&text=In%202021%2C%20there%20were%20approximately,during%20the%20COVID%2D19%20pandemic

In Singapore, elevators are called lifts. In the private condominium where we used to live, there were five lifts. Four had modern designs, and one was in a far corner, modest in appearance, and was designated as a service lift for maids, which always had a long queue. Our unit had its own maid's room, with a lock from outside the room. Outside of the maid's room was the laundry area and a small toilet for them to use. That room had no window to the outside but only a window for the employer to check on the maid.

I will focus my story on the lift.

I guessed I empathized with these maids because I also grew up on the farm like most of them. I also came from humble beginnings. I was fortunate enough to be educated like most of them. I also originally came from the Philippines. But for whatever reason, you can call it destiny or lack of a better opportunity, they ended up as maids.

Maids were not allowed to use the posh lifts. In my mind, should we isolate a certain group of individuals because of their job? Should we not allow them to use a common tool such as a lift if it does not pose any threat or disturbance to us?

In addition, with the condominium unit design, one could argue that the maid can be locked inside their room. That way, the maid will be afraid of the employer.

The element of instilling fear and authority— people who instill fear among those whom they have control over are not just evident with the way the maids in Singapore were treated. I also experienced it when I was active in academia and clinical practice.

I was called out one time concerning my style of teaching resident physicians, and these are younger physicians in-training. I was told that for the resident physicians to respect me, they should be afraid of me. I should instill fear in them so that they would not forget what I teach them. I should exert my authority and punish them if they do something unacceptable, like not joining me during my patient rounds.

I did the contrary, not because I wanted to defy authority but because I wanted to inspire the young physicians rather than instill fear among them. I was there to teach them the craft of doing surgical procedures. I was there to discuss with them how to manage their patients and have intellectual conversations on how difficult cases need to be managed. If nobody's life was ever compromised because of poor medical management, why would I punish young physicians while they were on their learning curve? Should I have gone with the flow and been strict with them so they would respect me? I was a young resident physician like them before.

I am a firm believer that respect is earned and should not be based on fear. Teaching should be based on values. Both of my parents are former educators, and I learned from them that the value of teaching using genuine care and understanding is more effective than instilling fear. Wouldn't it be more rewarding if we run across somebody we taught while they were young who will rush to us ecstatic and grateful when they see us? If we instilled fear, what is the likelihood that they will evade or stay away from us instead?

Just to get another perspective and not judge the system of our Singapore condo, I asked one of my neighbors concerning the service lift. The response was very practical. The main reason was that of cleanliness.

Maids usually come from the market, and some of the items they carry with them can smell, especially if those items come from the wet market. Or because of their work, they can be dirty hence the service lift. The service lift is also there for the utility workers to use because some of their tools can be filthy. The service lift was put in place to preserve the cleanliness of the building and the health of the occupants.

Those were good reasons why the service lift existed.

But what if the maid is not carrying anything from the wet market? What if the maid is clean?

I asked my neighbor to help me talk to the building administrator about it. If maids are clean and are not carrying anything that will compromise the cleanliness of the main lifts, they should be allowed to use them.

Since then, I have seen some of the maids use the main lifts.

In our life's journey, we go through certain phases whereby we may observe discrimination and feel other people's sense of isolation. One example is the maids' predicament in Singapore during that time when they were only allowed to use the service lifts. We may also encounter individuals who tell us to behave differently, such as my experience in academia and clinical practice, where I should impose authority and should be strict with the resident physicians.

But we need to consider the impact of such circumstances to other peoples' lives.

Maids will not be maids forever. They work as maids temporarily for a reason at a certain stage in their lives. More often than not, the main reason why they work as maids, even with college degrees, is to financially support their families in the Philippines and have better lives.

Residency training is not forever. The young physicians I was teaching the craft of Obstetrics and Gynecology to would not be residents forever. The main reason why one needs to be in training as a resident is to be a consultant in the future and have a better life.

As an expat, I had the opportunity to have a potential role in making a difference in somebody else's life. Will I make the life journey of other people painful? Should I rather make myself an instrument to help them with their plight? Should I make it less painful and support them so that they will succeed?

Some of you may say that such an approach may be abused. I agree. But there is such a thing as a Velvet Hammer type of leadership. I will go through it in detail in Chapter Ten.

During various stages in our lives, we may experience that feeling of seemingly being discriminated against or not accepted. It can happen regardless of our positions or roles in society. It can happen because of our gender, as I went through in detail in the preceding chapters. Sometimes we feel that whether it is a rule or not, whether it is the norm or not, we assume that we do not deserve to take the posh lift. Sometimes we feel obliged to give in to the demands of other people in authority, whether we are told or not, whether it is acceptable behavior or not, despite conflict with our values.

Sometimes, if we have conflict with individuals who make things hard for us, we end up leaving. We may give up rather than conquer that stage in our lives. Perhaps the easy way is to just leave. For the fighters among us, we may choose to stay.

At the end of the day, for those of us who choose to stay, is it worth it?

For those of us who choose to leave, did we make the right decision?

Whether you choose to stay or leave, such situations will change you. I know they did for me.

I left ...

I also stayed ...

In the next chapter, I will share my personal experiences of how I was pushed into a wall and what actions I took. The actions I took to manage such situations may come as a surprise to you.

So read on.

We have several more life lessons to reveal.

CHAPTER NINE

She Won't Last Long

Japan, Part Four

I had the privilege to return to Japan and work in the corporate world. I was given the opportunity to lead, manage, and develop a huge organization consisting of not just Japanese but also other nationalities. It was a humbling experience.

It was very rewarding as well since I am very passionate about developing young talents, not limited to women. For me, gender or race or religion should not be a determining factor for somebody to succeed. If I am an enabler of someone else's success, I will be one of the happiest human beings on earth. Just being somebody to someone is good enough for me.

I guess I was able to inspire not just women but also men in the workplace. I saw several of them shine and conquer the world. I saw some of them soar and reach their full potential and dreams.

When I returned, Japan made great strides. The country changed to a certain degree compared with the time when I relocated there for the first time. English is more frequently used, there are more foreigners, and there are initiatives to foster the welfare of women. This included dedicated "women only" cars in trains during peak hours of travel so that women would not be harassed during crowded commute times, among others.

Some of the Japanese became gradually comfortable communicating with others in English. The English language is very helpful in expressing one's ideas in a way that can be easily understood and not implied. My former assistant is very good at English, and she is not a typical reserved Japanese. I guess her fluency with the language made her more confident.

I previously mentioned that one of the things I love about Japan is that most people are respectful and honest. Wherever I go, I feel welcomed. In rare instances, though, I felt and sensed some sort of alienation to a certain degree. It may be because of differences with the language, race, or gender. For whatever reason, that feeling never disappeared.

What would you do if you were alienated or excluded because of your color, gender, or even because of the way you talk? Come to think of it, I am already a professional and occupied senior-level executive positions, yet I still felt I was not part of some conversations and felt excluded by particular behaviors or gestures. And this is not just a delusion. I am sure, in any way, shape, or form, you may have encountered situations whereby you felt like an outsider or you felt ill at ease because of a situation where you did not seem to belong at all. You may have felt the same way as I did.

I remember one time when somebody told me that it was preferred that I speak in Japanese because then I would be speaking politely and not directly. When I studied Japanese, I learned the plain, honorific, and polite forms and I used the latter more frequently. I prefer English not only because I was told to keep English as much as possible in the workplace but also because I am more comfortable with it. I can express what I really want to say. I guess I was not fair to those who were still struggling with the language. And perhaps I was just thinking of what was comfortable for me.

English can be blunt at times, with no implied meaning. The Japanese language can be tricky because sometimes the subject is implied. For example, to ensure that I am understood, I use a subject and not just the object or verb. I communicate using English, and I just don't inform. And to ensure that effective communication during business meetings did occur and that I was understood, I usually ask the other person to summarize or be clear with the necessary action that needed to be done after our conversation. I wanted to be on the fleet!

Conversations may at times become too formal in business, and sometimes, to avoid arguments, some of them end up saying "*Hai*," meaning "Yes," just to avoid further discussion. "Yes" may also be said to minimize the time spent listening or talking in English, especially for those who may still be uncomfortable with the language. "Yes" can also mean that not everything will be revealed, and some information will have to be buried. A common response I also got was "*Wakarimashita*," meaning "Understood." Was I really understood?

Being led by or having a woman as a manager can be challenging as well to the Japanese, let alone a foreigner. If I am a Japanese employee who is used to having a male manager, has the same nationality as me and is conversant with me in my native language, which is the standard, I would be very comfortable. If a woman becomes my manager who is from another country and talks with me in another language, I would be challenged as well.

So, I do understand what some of them are going through.

The trouble is, because I use English all the time, not everyone knows that I understand and speak the Japanese language. Otherwise, I would not have been granted the special license to practice medicine in Japan when I was there for the first time.

There was one time when I was walking in the hallway and overheard an unpleasant conversation in Japanese. The topic was about me. I was not aware that my comments were considered too direct and not understood. I did not know that the task I asked was impossible to be accomplished within a definite timeframe.

I should have known and asked for feedback.

At any rate, what stuck in my mind was the comment, "*Kanojo wa nagatsusuki shinai darou*," which means, "She won't last long!" I also heard the comment that "*Hai*" or "*Wakarimashita*" would be the responses that I would always get to stop me from talking any further but that nothing would be done anyway. And that I would not stay longer than three years, so who cares if the job is done or not? Three years is the usual duration of stay of most foreigners expatriated for work.

They also mentioned that they were just expressing themselves because I encouraged everyone to speak up, and they have been practicing how to do it. What I overheard made me realize that I needed to explain what the true essence of "Speak Up" actually is. It does not mean speaking behind other people's back just because you do not like the task given to you, or because you do not like the person.

That situation taught me to use feedback as much as possible. The feedback helped me ensure that I have visibility of my communication or behaviors that may impact others around me. It helped me become more self-aware and improve on areas that warrant improvement, such as the cultural appropriateness of my communication style.

Other situations where I felt alienated included comments along the lines of not knowing Japan enough and not knowing the culture enough. Comments to depict that I was not capable of doing the role assigned to me. And the worse comment of all was that I was not needed. That there should have been a Japanese man in my position. Work is already hard enough, so it shouldn't be made more difficult with the use of the English language. That would also provide them comfort because a Japanese would naturally know Japan better than a foreigner.

They would be more comfortable if they were led by a man.

They would be more comfortable if they were led by someone of their own kind.

They must have resented me.

Was it because I am a woman?

Was it because I am a foreigner?

Was it because I speak my mind or can be highly opinionated, especially in areas that I am very familiar with?

I must have talked a lot. Maybe I exuded a certain behavior that was too much for the Japanese society to take in.

I am the eldest daughter in the family and taking care of my five younger siblings when I was growing up made me resilient. I was raised by my grandmother on the farm since my mom was busy with her career. So maybe that, too, made me resilient.

The Filipino culture in me about resilience is the one that kept me going all along. If you are wondering whether you have met a Filipino, you may have had a conversation with one on the phone while talking with a customer call center agent. Or if you have embarked on a cruise or will do so in the near future, you have met or will most definitely meet a Filipino crewmember. One important element of our culture is to not give up easily. In fact, it is very rare to find depression among Filipinos because we always find a way to see the positive side of things. We laugh a lot, sing a lot, and dance a lot. We are engrossed in watching boxing matches and are truly entertained when Manny Pacquiao takes an opponent in the ring. We love to watch Miss Universe pageants because Filipino women end up bringing home the crown, such as Catriona Gray in 2018. We take pride in finding solutions to any problem.

Was everyone against me? No, it was only one percent. There is a Japanese occupying a high position who always had faith in me and enabled my success. He always made himself available when I needed support and always told me that my success was his success. My former manager, though based in Switzerland, mentored and helped me manage challenging situations.

I had my executive education course on medical bioinformatics, and part of it involved gene analysis. One of the interesting findings when I had my gene analyzed was that I have no empathy. I never realized that empathy could be determined using genetic analysis.

It crossed my mind that maybe the lack of empathy helped me to become resilient and strong. What is the limit of being resilient, though?

I always encourage people around me to speak up because I am a firm believer in it. It is encouraged to be used in a situation that is fundamentally unethical.

There was a time in my life when I spoke up, but that meant negatively impacting somebody in authority. What followed was a series of horrifying nightmares. I was subjected to psychological bullying, and there were a lot of unimaginable actions done by several people in authority. The psychological trauma was too much that I always had nightmares and cursed the start of every new day. That was because I knew it would just be another day of humiliation. I lost a lot of weight and was barely skin and bones. I was always jittery when I heard their voices. It was the only time when I dawdled eating because I wanted to minimize my exposure to them as much as possible.

During that time, I felt like an outsider. So there... I felt like an alien in a familiar culture and language that I could certainly relate to. I would say that even if we are in our own countries or comfort zones, one way or the other, we may feel some sort of alienation. We may feel alienated because we have been or are literally excluded. We may feel alienated because we feel we really do not belong.

Did I still belong? Definitely not.

Did I create the environment so as not to belong? Perhaps.

Was it me who created it though, or was it the fact that my core values were challenged; hence I did not belong?

Of course, as you can imagine, I questioned my decision to speak up during that time.

What if I didn't speak up and looked the other way? Would I live a happier life?

Would I be satisfied if I was treated well but buried a wrongdoing?

If I looked the other way, would I be able to sleep peacefully at night?

But would I be REALLY happy, in the true sense of my definition of happiness?

I am sure some of you may have been in similar situations in the past. Maybe you are trying to navigate through solutions as you may be experiencing one right now. I would be a fool to say that I was not affected by the bullying because I was.

Here are some more life lessons revealed ...

What did I do after hearing that I would not last long? I considered it a challenge. Did I retaliate? Definitely not. I showed by example.

Guess what? I kept going, I did not leave. I proved to others that I am very capable and that I will be able to stay longer than three years because I am highly motivated and passionate about what I do.

What kept me going was the fact that I discovered myself more. I was very much committed to developing young talents. And I was not alone. I had my family who supported me and made me realize how worthy of a person I am. I had my best friends who remained by my side and always made me laugh.

What did I do with the other situation? The situation where I was severely affected because of psychological bullying? Few people supported me and believed that what I did was right. Justice prevailed, which further reinforced the fact that I did the right thing. But I left.

I had to leave to regain my sanity.

I had to be there for my family and not exist for the bullies because they were not worth it.

I did not feel like I demonstrated defeat because I left. I felt that I won because I did the right thing.

I had to prioritize what mattered to me most.

So, if you are in a similar situation whereby others may not have faith in you or alienate you because of who you are or because you stand for what you truly believed in—know and define yourself.

Determine what matters most. Don't let others who are insignificant to you do that for you.

Know if something is too much.

Only YOU know YOU. You can be the better version, if not the best version of you. And that is the real best you!

Most importantly, if you need to speak up, just do it. Make sure that it is not meant to degrade anyone or do harm to others but to do good. The truth will always set you free.

Either way, whatever makes you content and satisfied because you can make a choice, and nobody can take that away from you.

All the experiences I had through the years made me a better person. It made me a better leader. What I am proud of is that there are no dead bodies left behind. And nobody died under my care as a physician, literally.

When I left Japan for the second time and returned to the U.S., I received a wonderful gift containing my picture on a canvas made from pictures of all the faces of my team members for the six years I spent there. In it was a note stating, "For being the leader that inspired us towards excellence and to always strive to be better than the best, your hard work and support shaped us to our current successful standing—we all wish to thank you, Jovelle. We will miss you very much." That gift said it all.

Was it worth it? Definitely.

Did I dedicate my energy to the one percent of individuals who made my life difficult? Of course not. I was not aspiring to be Miss Congeniality anyway. I dedicated my energy to those who needed me and those who deserved my attention, and that was ninety-nine percent.

Was I happy with my stay in Japan, not just once but twice? Absolutely. I would definitely love to return.

Japan changed me to be a better person and to become a better version of myself. Japan will always be my second home.

And I became a better leader that I know my dad would be proud of.

So what kind of a leader did I become? I became the velvet hammer.

CHAPTER TEN

The Velvet Hammer

U.S.

There was a recurring theme in my annual feedback while working in the corporate world. That recurring theme involved my leadership style. I seek for help rather than reprimand, especially when managing problematic situations or behaviors.

At one point, one of my former managers referred to me as "The Velvet Hammer." It seems that I have a way of carefully using words appropriate enough not to hurt other people's feelings but firm enough to get the job done. The type of delivery of my communication is soft like velvet but has an "umph." It is like saying to the other person you are stupid without using the word or anything similar in the conversation.

Speaking of my communication style, somebody pointed out one time that I needed to correct my accent. I was taken aback and never thought that something was wrong with it to begin with. I responded back by saying, "So which one is the right accent?" I did not get any response back. I believe that as long as I am understood well, and that I will be able to deliver my message across effectively and efficiently, does accent really matter?

Later, I came across a book by Joy Baldridge, the author of *The Joy in Business: Innovative Ideas to Find Positivity (and Profit) in Your Daily Work Life.* She illustrated the velvet hammer approach method in her book with a formula. Condoleeza Rice, the former U.S. National Security Adviser, was highlighted as someone who has a profile of a velvet hammer. She was described as someone who can be harsh and understanding depending on the circumstances.

So how did I become a velvet hammer?

Restless discontent is something that never escapes me. In other words, there is always room to learn and improve. There is always room to become a better person and have better deliverables. I never stopped learning. In fact, I am always thirsty to learn something new such as with my Executive Education Programs.

In other words, I won't stop to continue to develop a better version of myself.

Let me share the velvet side ...

I was told that even when it was just my second day in the office, many of the people in the office already knew me. I smiled to almost everyone I met. I wanted to make the other person feel better, and a smile usually starts a good conversation and a good impression. I may have started the "smile pandemic." I had an open-door policy so everyone could just come and discuss with me if they had any challenges where they may have needed my advice. I ensured that others had the tools they needed to succeed and encouraged them to speak up as appropriate. I became a confidant in some situations. I came to know some of my team member's family circumstances. So much so that I would tell them to go home when it was past office hours. That way, they could take care of their families. They could help their wives tend to their children. They could take care of their ailing parents. I became not just their manager but also their friend and confidante. They knew that I had their backs when they got into trouble. They knew that I would support them to become better at their job. They knew that I would be considerate of their situations. They knew that I would promote them if they deserved it, even if they would just come back from maternity leave. They knew that I respected them as human beings and that I was cognizant of their needs and did not just treat them as subordinates.

And the hammer side ...

I always set up realistic objectives and took into account that the deliverables had to be met, if not exceeded. I knew those deliverables were doable, manageable, and could be done within the specified period of time because all the necessary resources were provided. I also ensured that they were trained and capable of doing the work. So much so that majority of my team members were mindful of their deliverables. They prepared themselves well when they made presentations to me to make sure that I understood what they wanted to communicate. They knew I did not tolerate unethical and senseless behavior. For some reason, I was able to instill fear without intending to do so to the extent that they became familiar with my footsteps when I walked in the hallway, a signal that they should be ready.

I can be nice, but at the same time, I can be strict.

I can empathize, but I cannot be fooled.

It is hard for me, though, to be like Manny Jacinto, who played Jason in "The Good Place." I struggle to just be a fly on the wall. It is unheard of for me to just be quiet. I am happy with the reactions of people around me when I do or give them something. Maybe like what Bretman Rock felt when he gave a gift to a sister, Princess. I always lend a helping hand because I know we are all working for the same cause. And that is always centered on patients. The needs of patients are prioritized. Patient first.

Did I become too "velvety"? I guess I also did. I was placed in very difficult situations, not just once but several times, by people I developed, trained, and trusted. But did that change me? I continued to develop, train, and trust people. Some of you may say that I never learned. But you know what? I always see the uniqueness and good in people. There is always something fundamentally good that just needs to be cultivated in others. If the good in them is harnessed, they will be better than their best selves. Their real best selves. They can be heroes, too, because they will be given a chance to make a difference in other people's lives.

Did I ever have challenging situations and conversations about being a velvet hammer? Yes, I did. And this is where the foreplay will be useful, which I will describe in the last chapter.

One of my primary school best friends once told me that she already knew I had the making of a leader. This was because I wanted to take the lead. I wanted to take control. She said I might have been influenced by my mom, who led huge organizations during her career. I did not think of myself as a leader growing up. I just wanted to have more friends.

Are leaders born?

Are they developed?

There is no secret formula for being a leader.

Being a leader does not mean being followed by several people or being popular. Being a leader does not mean you have control over many people or have several people reporting to you.

We all have different definitions of a leader.

I think being a leader means being someone who motivates and brings out the best in others. For me, the keyword I affiliate with a leader is "inspiration." A leader will always consider that authentic encouragement is important. Genuine care is important. Leadership is all about continuously learning and adapting.

Adam Grant, the author of *Think Again*, elaborated on the ability to rethink and unlearn. I found it powerful because there is a lot of learning about leadership. I let go of knowledge and opinions that were not advantageous to me. There were some solutions I needed to rethink, and it gave me the opportunity to come up with better solutions to problems.

Additionally, leadership is about people. Flexibility in the leadership style is also important. Some people may need to be hammered. Some people may need a gentle touch. Some may just need a slight nudge. Whatever the leadership style, it is important to have clarity on why you are doing it. You need to explain the why behind it. You need to understand what the other person is really telling you. You need to really listen.

Tough? Yes... of course. Being a leader is not easy.

Being expatriated molds one to be a better leader because of the learnings one can get dealing with various situations, cultures, and personalities.

And sometimes, when you are given a tough problem that needs to be managed, think of your values and your faith. That is why there is BTS.

CHAPTER ELEVEN

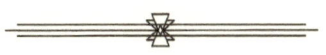

BTS

Virtual universe

The COVID-19 pandemic was unprecedented and created a huge impact on society, the people, to all of us. Behaviors changed, some of them radically.

Working remotely became the norm. Virtual events became more common, and the lesser the contact with another human being, the better. In fact, I had my own avatar which I used to communicate to my team members and provide presentations during speaking engagements. I guess some, if not most of you, also had to adjust your lifestyles. Perhaps you started a new hobby? Or maybe learned a new recipe? The pandemic made all of us reflect on our lives and made us reevaluate ourselves.

Because I had to stay indoors, the pandemic made me do a lot of binge-watching instead of strolling at the parks during weekends. Netflix, Hulu, HBO Max, and Amazon Prime Video became my new best buddies. I laughed a lot and watched "Friends" like a gazillion times, cried a lot watching "This is Us," was horrified with "Stranger Things," and became super emotional with "Handmaid's Tale." I guess some of you started to do binge-watching as well. I dare say that apart from the remote way of working, binge-watching also became the norm.

I became addicted to the YouTube videos of Selena Gomez when she was roasted by Gordon Ramsay and that of Dwayne Johnson when he was teaching his daughter to say that he is the best. I watched Ellen with my family during meals and loved her parting words during every show, "Be kind to one another." I listened to Oprah's Supersoul podcasts every morning, and those podcasts inspired me and helped me understand the value and meaning of life. I also improved my cooking skills thanks to Jamie Oliver's videos. I learned other areas I was not familiar with, such as those from the amazing videos done by my architect nephew, Llyan Oliver Austria.

I also had to attend mass virtually.

I attend the virtual masses officiated by Rev. Fr. Jerry Orbos. I attend his masses not because I came from Pangasinan like Fr. Jerry but because I am deeply moved by his inspirational homily and his relatable teachings.

Fr. Jerry is known for using acronyms to deliver his messages. He repeatedly mentions BTS. It stands for Believe Trust Surrender.

It did not mean BTS or Bangtan Boys, a famous South Korean boy band.

BTS strengthened my faith that I will overcome whatever challenges I am facing—whether that pertains to something at work, something related to family and friends, or something related to me. It is very applicable in any situation.

BTS became my tool.

Believe ...

Trust ...

Surrender ...

Of course, my faith is strengthened every time I watch the movie "The Passion of the Christ." In fact, I always made it a point to watch the movie with my family every Lenten season. I already knew the story, and I needed to have a box of facial tissues within arm's reach to wipe the endless tears. But I still wanted to watch it repeatedly.

You can just imagine my frustration when I had to make a business trip during the Lenten season. Because my time was very constrained, I would not have the chance to watch the movie.

My routine... disrupted by work. That was not the first time. Some of you may have encountered a routine disrupted by work. You must have felt frustrated as well.

Well, there is that expression, "You've got to do what you've got to do."

So anyway, reluctantly, I had to make that trip. I had to spend the Lenten season attending a meeting rather than observing lent. Nonetheless, I was able to do a meatless fast and hurried prayers. I felt so guilty because I felt like I was not able to fulfill my Catholic obligations to the fullest.

I should have told you that the business meeting was in Rome, Italy. I figured I could celebrate lent in Rome and visit St. Peter's Basilica in Vatican City. And some of you may say, "Rome during lent? Come on! You should be grateful!"

Yes, I was indeed grateful because another memorable incident happened on the way to Rome.

I had the chance to sit near the person who played Jesus in the movie, Jim Caviezel. I usually do not start conversations on the plane because I am too engrossed with work. But that was the only instance when I did not open my laptop or browse my notes. I had the chance to chat with Jim.

I started the conversation by mentioning my frustration concerning missing the movie. He was so polite and engaging, and he showed pictures of him while doing the movie. He said that it would make me feel better if he would share some of his experiences while filming the movie. I felt so privileged and ecstatic. I got to watch the movie from another perspective. I cried as well because I got to revisit scenes that moved me.

Talk about BTS ...

Believe.

Trust.

Surrender.

Many people say that physicians are the worst patients. Maybe because we are familiar with the art of medicine. Maybe we tend to lose subjectivity if we are the ones involved.

With the stressful life that I had, and with less opportunity to exercise or even have a work-life balance, you can just imagine how that took a toll on my health. Of course, there are other factors apart from lifestyle, such as genetics.

Anyway, the added benefit of being an expat was that my family and I received the best healthcare services one could ever get. This is true regardless of the country we were living in or the country we traveled to. That is also a good privilege altogether of working in very good companies.

Indulge me with the next story.

With lingering symptoms that I will not normally associate with something severe, I just visited the outpatient department of a hospital expecting to receive better medicines than those that can be bought over the counter. I was expecting to go back home and resume work. The resident physician made referrals to various specialists, and I was not aware that I was already suffering from a very severe condition. So severe that I needed to be admitted to the intensive care unit and receive tons of medications and so many diagnostic procedures. So severe that I was also scheduled for a very difficult and potentially life-threatening surgery.

I put a halt on my much-needed surgical intervention.

Maybe I was too afraid to be subjected to the knife... or maybe I was not thinking straight because the pre-surgery medication was already kicking in. Or maybe I knew that the surgery itself was complicated to perform.

While I was being wheeled to the operating room, I told the hospital patient transporter to stop. I asked him to call the surgeon. He said the surgeon was already waiting inside the operating room. I repeated my request. I told him that I needed to talk to the surgeon again because I had to tell him something important. Surgeon-to-surgeon talk was needed. He obliged.

The surgeon came and spoke to me. He heard the most unbelievable request from a patient.

I asked him, "Have you ever felt that something is not right prior to an operation?"

He said yes.

"And because something was not right, did you ever decide not to proceed?"

He made a long pause and did not answer back.

I paused and took a deep breath before I uttered the next words. "I feel something is not right. I am not challenging the diagnosis or the management of my case. I just feel something. Not because I am a patient but because I did have this feeling before. And what I did in that situation was not to perform the surgery. And I made the right decision for that case. I am asking you, therefore, not to proceed with my surgery."

I guess I sounded so convincing because he did not argue at all. He explained that I just needed to sign a waiver which I complied.

A few months after that, that same surgeon told me that my life-threatening condition, which should have been treated by surgery, was miraculously healed. The impossible happened. Just like that! Thank you, Lord! Jesus, I trust in You! Mama Mary, I love You!

I am not saying that I didn't trust my attending physicians. I did. I am not saying that you should not have your disease treated because it will go away. I am not saying that before you are subjected to any operation, you need to find that discomfort and refuse surgery.

I am not saying that maybe my diagnostic results were switched with someone else's. We did check everything. Physicians are even extra careful when they manage fellow physicians as their patients. My husband and I were included in the discussions when we were diagnosing my case and decided on the best management.

Until today, I cannot explain what happened to me. I cannot explain it despite all the research I did concerning my case.

Were the visits to Our Lady of Manaoag in the Philippines or Our Lady of Fatima in Portugal helpful? Was it the fact that I fervently prayed each and every day and trusted in Jesus and Mama Mary? Was it because I offered prayers in every church I visited in every country? Was it because I always joined the anointing of the sick in the church?

How about a change in my lifestyle?

How about the fact that I became a very obedient patient? From the medications to the doctor consultations and follow-ups...

Did those make a difference?

BTS ...

Believe.

Trust.

Surrender.

"Wherever we are, whatever we are going through," as Rev. Fr. Jerry Orbos would always say, "BTS."

So, whatever situation I was in... Always BTS, and in all ways, BTS.

It enabled me to overcome whatever came my way.

Was that enough, though?

Read on ...

CHAPTER TWELVE

The Foreplay

Five countries relocated and lived in.
Fifty countries traveled.

D on't get me wrong.
My definition here of foreplay is not what most of you may think.

Foreplay in this chapter is an action or behavior that precedes an event.

The action or behavior is a better understanding of each other's needs through good communication. The event is the creation of a long-lasting relationship and gives satisfaction to both parties.

When you uproot yourself from a seemingly familiar environment to an unfamiliar territory, it can be daunting. It is not just stressful for you but also for your family if you bring them along with you. Your children's schooling will be potentially disrupted. They will be away from their familiar school and their friends. Your spouse will need to find a new job that will be aligned with his or her career plans. If you used to live close to your parents, that would also take your time away from them.

Living in other countries certainly can be exciting, but it can be intimidating, too.

When we lived in Singapore, we felt inferior at some point since the image of Filipinos in Singapore is that of a domestic helper. When we lived in Belgium, we felt we did not belong because we were not taken seriously by the police when our house was burglarized. When we lived in Japan, we felt alienated because we behaved differently, and there were norms and standards that were difficult to comprehend. When we first migrated to the U.S., my attention was called out one time because I was not speaking "well," and that person explained that it had something to do with my accent. When we lived in the Philippines, I felt alienated because I was pushed into a corner and did not scratch somebody else's back because I had to do the right thing.

Traveling to various places can bring so much fun, but it can be stressful, too.

Part of my work entails a lot of traveling, both domestic and international. I must attend meetings and meet various individuals. In addition, I must adjust as well with my communication style to ensure that I am understood and successfully deliver what I need to do. I have loved every minute of it since every travel experience for me makes me wonder in amazement. It was like the excitement I had when I was still active in performing surgical procedures and that no two cases are alike. There is always something different and unique, even if the travel is to the same city, making it thrilling and all the more interesting.

When I encountered challenging situations living and traveling in different countries, I wondered if there must be something fundamentally wrong with me because maybe, just maybe, I was trying too hard to fit in.

I guess I was losing my essence and value as a person.

Well, I had to have a good grip on my culture and my true self to overcome the challenges involving relocation and travel. I had to find a way and never give up. Because I am focused. Because I am driven. Because I have something valuable to offer to others. I should be proud of my culture because that will enable me to keep on moving. I should not be affected by stressful elements around me.

As Ghita Filali puts it, there is that cultural prism whereby apart from our own personal culture, we have our country's culture, and when we join an organization, there is another culture as well. When we communicate, we bring our own perspectives, which could be highly influenced by our own culture or at least our perception of things based on our culture as a person, as a citizen of a country, and as a person working in an organization. We can, and I dare say, at least try or should adjust the way we communicate. We need to take into account the recipient of that communication.

So how did foreplay apply to me in a practical way in the various countries I got expatriated? Maybe I will be able to illustrate it better if I share how I lived my life on a normal, uneventful day.

Imagine a multiverse, and you are with me in the Philippines, Singapore, Japan, Belgium, and the U.S.—countries where I lived and worked.

Let us start with me leaving my place.

After eating breakfast, I rush through traffic in the Philippines while having a meeting inside the car. I take the bus and train in Singapore, but there is so much noise around, so I had to use headphones. I take the train in Japan with similar people I see in the same train car, and the train is always on time, so I will never be late. I drive a car on a scenic path to the office in Belgium. I join a carpool in the U.S. while traversing the highway.

Upon arrival at the office, there are some differences. The security personnel in the Philippines will smile and will politely let you in. Those in Japan will bow and greet you good morning. Personnel at the entrance in the U.S. will have a casual conversation with you about the weather or about sports.

There is, obviously, a difference involving the office layout and with the company personnel that I see and work with.

Lunch can be different as well. Cafeteria food is basically similar to what you can find in other cafeterias in that country. Food in Japan is healthy, and there is always green tea. Lunch in Singapore can be at the hawkers. In any country, lunch meetings are common.

After office hours, coming home is with the same mode of transportation as going to the office.

Whatever multiverse I am in, whichever country I got expatriated to, I always come home to the same person. My sons may be there or not, as they may be in school. But what remains constant is always my husband.

Foreplay... a process.

Because of constant interaction with colleagues, I was able to understand their needs and create long-lasting relationships with them. Good communication is key.

Communication is always tricky because, at times, we may think that we communicated well but what we did was just inform. We may neglect to consider the receiver of the information and miss being understood. Communication should not be limited to a few. It could be with the relevant people I work with, with the individuals I meet with, or with those whom I collaborate with. I need to make sure that I am understood. I need to make sure that I pay particular attention to their needs and their situations. I need to make sure that I understand them. And I need to adjust my communication style based on their circumstances.

Unless there is urgency or something high-risk in nature is being managed...

Do I say "Merry Christmas" to my team or colleagues from various places in the world during the holiday season? No. I need to say "Happy Holidays" to be mindful of Hanukkah, Eid, and Kwanzaa.

Do I schedule meetings that may be contrary to other religious beliefs, such as Sabbath, or even culture, such as siesta? No. I need to be considerate of the other person's practices.

If I have meetings with several individuals located in many countries, such that time difference can be an issue, do I always schedule it such that the time is suitable only for me? No. I need to make sure that I am respectful of their "me time." I need to ensure everyone is comfortable and at least take turns to work beyond office hours so that work will not be that disruptive to their families and their personal lives.

I treated others that way because that was how I wanted to be treated. Even if the other person did not ask, I would certainly make it a point to respect his or her time because I expect him or her to do the same to me.

I believe that is how the foreplay needs to be made—being aware of the situation of the other and being understanding. I did it that way, and I was able to build good relationships with colleagues in the process. Giving satisfaction and being satisfied.

Satisfaction for me is that I get the job done because I communicate well.

What and who else needs to be satisfied?

I need to satisfy my personal life as well. I need to make sure that my husband, Daddy Alex is happy. I need to make sure that he can also move forward with his career and be fulfilled. I need to make sure that my sons, AJ, Justin and Alex are happy. I need to make sure that they develop themselves more, learn to be resilient, and be more knowledgeable about the world around them.

Personally, the experiences that came along with being expatriated honed me with an essential perspective that made me whole and become a better person. I became closer to my husband, akin to the Neo and Trinity love in "The Matrix Insurrection," and bound with the love of the family such that the "I'll Be There" song of the Jackson 5 is cruising through our veins.

Did I feel satisfied all the time when I was an expat? Nope …

I had regrets. I missed several important events in school. I felt guilty when I was not present for my family. By "being present," I was referring to both mind and body. There were times when I spent vacations with my family, but I was constantly thinking of work. There were times when I was not supporting my husband enough because I was too preoccupied with the decisions I made at work. There were times when I wasn't really listening to my sons when they shared what happened to them during one given day. I lived far from my parents, and my communication with them became less and less.

I missed big extended family gatherings laden with so much food because I needed to travel. I missed meeting my girlfriends for our usual Friday night healthy routines because I got relocated. I missed chatting face to face with my mom about almost anything. I missed my dad.

Will I take all my experiences as an expat or with my travels as just things of the past? Will I choose to live in the past and hate myself with those regrets? Or will I choose to live in the current moment?

I choose to live in the current moment. I choose to dedicate as much time as possible to things that matter to me most. I choose to live in the current moment using the learnings from the experiences from the past.

The relocation and travels to various countries definitely changed me.

Are there more life lessons of being an expat and a million miler that need to be revealed?

The life lessons came along with the adventure. It enriched me to understand the perspective of others, whether from another culture, another country, or another language. I learned to understand the perspective of others, even if they have similar culture as mine.

Seeing my sons become more responsible and highly adaptable always makes me smile. Their independence and drive to fulfill their dreams are astounding. Their exposures to every possibility are exceptional. Their family values are so rich.

My love for my husband grew deeper, and our relationship was reinforced. And our faith in God became stronger.

Living in various countries made us rely on each other more because we needed to live through the complexities of being a foreigner. The life lessons we gained through those years will forever be cherished because those learnings made us better people.

The bond of our family became stronger.

Ahh... I made the right decision to be an expat!

Just look at that significant person beside you. That person may have mixed feelings as well, just like you do. Start communicating. Build or strengthen a relationship.

Start the foreplay!

Epilogue

As an expat, there are intangible benefits that I personally treasure, and those are the life lessons that will never be forgotten. Living in another country enabled my family and me to adapt and learn new culture and new language. Those experiences created a lot of insane but true stories as well that made us wonder in amazement or just laugh out loud. Of course, we also experienced countless challenges since being a foreigner is not that easy.

Living in those countries enabled my sons to be highly versatile, and they made several friends from all around the world. In fact, at one point, my eldest son, AJ, responded to a question about citizenship with, "I am a citizen of the world," rather than, "I am a citizen of the U.S.," because of his experiences living and studying in various countries.

What about my dearest husband? He found a way to optimize those relocations by developing himself and devoting his efforts to things that inspired and motivated him. In fact, he gained a lot of expertise with investments and the stock market such that he is often asked by friends and acquaintances what he did to optimize his returns. In addition, he became passionate about beautifying our home!

Whether you are or will be expatriated to another country, are relocated or will be relocated to an unfamiliar place, are traveling or will travel to another place...

Whether you stay put but will encounter a new person or a new situation...

Your core values may be challenged, or you may feel alienated.

With any new, unfamiliar place, unfamiliar culture, unfamiliar language ...

Mixed emotions will always be there. Questions as to what you need to say or do will always linger.

Just remember the life lessons I shared in this book.

Were there times when I was impulsive and made bad decisions? Sure.

Were there times when I made mistakes? Definitely.

Were there times when I lost the real me in the process? Absolutely.

Did I ever feel a bazinga moment? Duh.

You know what? You will be fine!

Be driven by your values. Continue to define yourself.

You can control your actions and behaviors in any situation... and you have options all the time. You can choose to do the right thing guided by your values. You can walk away, or you can dance to the music and pretend. Either way, whatever makes you happy and satisfied. You do not need to have superpowers to make a difference in this world. You can be a hero!

Of course, whatever you do, whatever decision you make, you may not be right all the time. At least try to be well-informed before you make decisions.

Always keep in mind that you are important. Your core values will guide you to manage whatever challenges you have.

Don't let toxic people get inside your head. Smile and tell yourself this, "I am beautiful, I am awesome, and I will always stay that way." Remember that cosmetic surgery and anti-aging products are very expensive.

Prioritize what matters most. Prioritize YOU.

And you know what? You are not alone. Help is always available. All you need to do is ask—whether that involves a person in authority or position who genuinely cares, or most importantly, whether that help will come from your loved ones.

Communicate with the right people at the right time and be clear about the ask. Don't just sit in a corner and wait for others to notice you. Instead, let others know that you exist.

Most importantly, have faith.

These are the reflections and life lessons that helped me shape the person I am today. I became the better, if not the best, version of myself.

Who knows? You may end up a better version, if not the best version, of yourself, too.

Bibliography

1. https://jokoy.com/

2. https://www.dictionary.com/

3. https://en.wikipedia.org/wiki/
   Thor:_Love_and_Thunder

4. Eisenberg E. (2021). *Bridesmaids' Famous
   Food Poisoning Scene Cut out a Spectacularly
   Gross Moment.* Retrieved from https://
   www.cinemablend.com/news/2567549/
   bridesmaids-famous-food-poisoning-
   scene-cut-spectacularly-gross-moment

5. Golembewski V. (2015) *The Surprising
   Success Rate of "How YOU Doin'?"* Retrieved
   from https://www.refinery29.com/
   en-us/2015/09/93481/joey-friends-pick-up-lines

6. https://en.wikipedia.org/wiki/Onsen

7. https://en.wikipedia.org/wiki/Hammam

8. https://www.statista.com/topics/6994/
    crime-in-the-philippines/#dossierKeyfigures

9. https://www.belgium.be/en/
    about_belgium/tourism

10. https://multiculturalcookingnetwork.
    wordpress.com/2009/12/27/
    vanessa-hudgens-loves-filipino-food/

11. https://worldpopulationreview.com/
    country-rankings/happiest-countries-in-the-world

12. https://www.countryliving.com/life/
    a39155616/mother-teresa-quotes/

13. https://psa.gov.ph/statistics/survey/
    labor-and-employment/survey-overseas-
    filipinos#:~:text=The%20number%20of%20
    Overseas%20Filipinos,2.18%20million%20
    reported%20in%202019.&text=The%20
    number%20of%20Overseas%20Contract,from%20
    2.11%20million%20in%202019.

14. https://asiasociety.org/philippines/
    lessons-suze-orman

15. https://www.moj.go.jp/MINJI/en/entop.html

16. https://en.wikipedia.org/wiki/
    When_I_Was_Your_Man

17. https://en.wikipedia.org/wiki/
    Someone_like_You_(Adele_song)

18. https://en.wikipedia.org/wiki/
    Family_Portrait_(song)

19. https://www.sumo.or.jp/En/

20. https://www.cnn.com/2018/04/05/asia/
    japan-sumo-women-ring-emergency-
    intl-trnd#:~:text=Maizuru%20city%20
    Mayor%20Ryozo%20Tatami,the%20
    ring%2C%20which%20they%20did.

21. https://www.nytimes.com/2000/03/26/
    world/governor-butts-heads-with-
    sumo-ban-on-women.html

22. https://www.weforum.org/reports/global-gender-
    gap-report-2022/digest/#:~:text=North%20
    America%20leads%20all%20regions,72.6%25%20
    of%20its%20gender%20gap.

23. https://www.reuters.com/article/
    olympics-2020-mori-int/tokyo-2020-chief-
    mori-makes-sexist-remarks-at-games-
    meeting-newspaper-idUSKBN2A325Z

24. https://www.unwomen.org/en/news/in-focus/
    women-and-the-sdgs/sdg-4-quality-education

25. https://www.usaid.gov/what-we-do/
gender-equality-and-womens-empowerment

26. https://en.wikipedia.org/wiki/
Extraordinary_Attorney_Woo

27. https://www.statista.com/statistics/953137/
singapore-foreign-domestic-workers-
employed/#:~:text=Number%20of%20
foreign%20domestic%20workers%20in%20
Singapore%202013%2D2021&text=In%202021%2C%-
20there%20were%20approximately,during%20
the%20COVID%2D19%20pandemic.

28. Baldrige JD. (2019). *The Joy in Business: Innovative Ideas to Find Positivity (and Profit) in Your Daily Work Life.* New York, NY: Wiley.

29. Edmonds R. (2004). *Condoleezza Rice: Profile of a "Velvet Hammer."* Retrieved from https://www.nbcnews.com/id/wbna4684024

30. https://thegoodplace.fandom.
com/wiki/Manny_Jacinto

31. https://www.youtube.com/
watch?v=_8jKHX16TNA&ab_
channel=TiktokVideos

32. Grant A. (2021). *Think Again.* New York, NY: Penguin Random House.

33. https://www.yahoo.com/video/selena-gomez-squirms-gordon-ramsay-142555166.html

34. https://www.facebook.com/ESPNUK/videos/the-rock-his-daughter-%EF%B8%8F/1071092160059280/

35. https://www.ellentube.com/

36. https://www.oprah.com/app/super-soul-sunday.html

37. https://www.jamieoliver.com/recipes/category/books/jamies-30-minute-meals/

38. https://en.wikipedia.org/wiki/Llyan_Oliver_Austria

39. https://divinewordmedia.com/fr-jerry-orbos-svd-video-collection-2/

40. Personal communication, Ghita Filali Coaching, LLC

Acknowledgments

Writing this book made me realize that I have so many people in my life that helped mold me into who I am today. My husband, sons, and dog are my ultimate secrets because they made me a "better than the best" version of myself. I also want to take this opportunity to thank the following individuals who inspired me throughout my extraordinary journey. I may have missed some names, but you know who you are.

The amazing people in the house—my dad Joven (RIP), mom Julie, siblings, in-laws, nieces, nephews, uncles, aunties, and cousins in all the corners of this planet earth, whether on air, land, or sea

My ever-supportive former managers and mentors, especially Masato Iwasaki, Pierre Pellier, Bill Sigmund, Hans Bock, Jane Wynen, Hugues Bogaerts, Sandy Macrae, Reddie Sumpaico, Ces Ladines, Raul Quillamor, Beth Dacanay, Veeh Balajo, Chit Dizon, Mildred Ayson, Takeshi and Keiko Maruo, Hiroya Matsuo, Satoru Motoyama, Ikuo Seguchi, and other professors, staff, and alumni of Kobe University and Saint Louis University

My spiritual advisers—Fr. Mario Colina, Fr. Efren Esmilla, Fr. Gelo Gazzingan, Fr. Ariel Tecson, and other Rogationist priests

My "always there for me" BFFs, czters, Philly Pinoy friends, and Healthcare Businesswomen's Association and Chief sisters, especially Anna Hamada, Andy Laranang, Joyce Garcia, Tonette Quinsaat, Olivia Ledres, Yuki Suga, Chiyo Aoshima, Rhoda Delizo, Malou Villanueva, Glynis Gregorio, Regz Montanez, Mitch Iko, Rachel Hinlo, Aileen Arquitola, Kathy Bo, Neriza Saito, Libay Suzuki, Rhea Manniquis, Cel Cascolan, Ollie Chua, Raquel Lopez, Tita Francisco, Chie Kawamori, Cris Bolaton, Sheryl Celino, Gen Recolizado, Karla Rillera, Ruth Taguiling, Ina Crisologo, Yuko Miyata, Beth Perez, Glo David, Dina Ymana, Gina Lavarias, Ethel Bautista, Vivian Sebastian, Joni Kollmer, Jennifer Moon, Chiyoko Kawakami, Miyo Miyagawa, and Rachel Yokota

My "always make me laugh" guy pals, especially Mar Macaltao, Willy Tibayan, Joey Garcia, Francis Del Val, Tony Herrera, Mario Sanchez, Koki Nakamura, Akira Iwakawa, Kurt Rimkus, Eufrael Bachar, Adrian Verueco, Choo-Beng Goh, Nonnie Bautista, and Toshiro Shirakawa

My super smart professors from the Executive Education of Wharton School of Business and the wonderful staff, fellow alumni, and my awesome Wharton Alumni Leadership buddies

The good people of Mangatarem, Pangasinan, and Baguio City, Philippines, Singapore, Belgium, Kobe, and Tokyo, Japan

...and the list goes on

About the Author

J ovelle Fernandez is a wife, a mother, a daughter, a sister, and a friend who highly values relationships. She lived in several countries (U.S., Japan, Singapore, Belgium, Philippines) to assume roles of increasing leadership with various scopes (global, regional, and country levels) while working at a couple of big pharma. Jovelle obtained M.D. from the Philippines, Ph.D. from Japan and executive education programs from the U.S., Netherlands, UK and Singapore. She received various accolades from the academia—Japan Society of Obstetrics and Gynecology and Asia Oceania Federation of Obstetrics and Gynecology. She also received Heritage *Pamana ng Pilipino* Award from the President of the Philippines and the Rising Star award from the Healthcare Businesswomen Association. She served as a speaker and panelist in various international academic and pharmaceutical industry settings, such as the World Economic Forum 4th Industrial Revolution. She is one of the founding members and is on the Executive Board, and serves as the Chief Operations Officer (COO) of Immunorock, Co. Ltd, a company that is developing an oral cancer vaccine. She is a visiting professor at Kobe University Graduate School of Science, Technology and Innovation. Jovelle is passionate about mentoring, training, and coaching individuals; hence, she established her own consulting company aimed at developing better than the best teams and individuals in the healthcare industry. She lives in Henderson, Nevada, with her family and Mochi, the beloved family dog. For more information, visit www.jovellefernandez.authorchannel.co

www.ingramcontent.com/pod-product-compliance
Lightning Source LLC
Chambersburg PA
CBHW050856150626
46549CB00013B/2420